BUSY BOOKS BIBLE STUDIES

FOR KIDS AGES 8-12

MADISON & DARLENE SCHACHT

TIME-WARP WIFE MINISTRIES

Busy Books: Bible Studies for Kids

Publisher:
Time-Warp Wife Ministries
Suite 5-1377 Border Street
Winnipeg, Manitoba R3H ON1

Interior design by Madison Schacht
Cover design by Darlene Schacht

Interior images provided by Bigstock.com Cover image by Dibustock.com

ISBN 978-1-988984-11-7

What We'll be Learning...

In the next few weeks we are going to be studying a few different stories in the Bible and getting to know them a bit better. Here's a list of the topics we're going to study:

OLD TESTAMENT

The Book of Genesis

The Beginning
Noah and the Ark
The Tower of Babel

The Book of Exodus

The Birth of Moses
Moses and the Burning Bush
The Ten Plagues on Egypt
The Ten Commandments

The Book of Esther

Esther and Mordecai

The Book of Daniel

Daniel in the Lions' Den

The Book of Jonah

Jonah and the Big Fish

NEW TESTAMENT

The Book of Luke

The Birth of Jesus
Zacchaeus Meets Jesus

The Book of John

Jesus Turns Water into Wine
The Parable of the Lost Sheep

The Book of Galatians

The Fruit of the Spirit

The Book of Ephesians

Armor of God

PUT ON THE FULL ARMOR OF GOD, SO THAT YOU CAN TAKE YOUR STAND AGAINST THE DEVILS SCHEMES.

- Ephesians 6:11, NIV -

I am with you and
will watch over you
wherever
you go
Genesis 28:15A, NIV

THE BOOK OF GENESIS

This week we are learning about...

The Beginning

You probably know the story of creation. In the beginning, God created the heavens and the earth. Before then everything was formless and darkness covered the surface of everything.

On the first day God said "Let there be light," and there was light. He saw it was good and separated it from the darkness. He called the light "day," and He called the darkness "night."

On the second day God created the sky. He said "Let there be a vault between the waters to separate water from water."

God commanded "let the water under the sky be gathered to one place, and let dry ground appear." And on the third day God named the dry ground "land," and He named the waters "seas." Then God said "Let the land produce vegetation: seed-bearing plants and trees on the land that bear fruit with seed in it, according to their various kinds." And on the third day God created both the land and its plants and trees.

On the fourth day, God created the sun, the moon, and the stars. He said, "I will make lights in the sky to separate the day from the night, and they will serve as signs to mark sacred times and days and years, and let them give light to the earth." God made two different lights, the sun to watch over the day and the moon and stars to watch over the night.

The fifth day, God created all of the living creatures on the earth and in the sea. The creation of all the animals were done.

On the sixth day God created mankind. He created them in His own image, male and female. God blessed them and said to them, "Be fruitful and increase in number; fill the earth and rule over it."

He put them in charge of the fish in the sea and the birds in the sky and over every living creature that moves on the ground. These were also given to man for food. And to all the animals of the earth and all the birds in the sky and all other creatures - everything that breaths - God gave them plants for food.

God was pleased with what He made and saw that it was good. And on the sixth day God had finished creating the heavens and the earth.

Read through **Genesis 1:1-31**

DAY ONE

Today's Date: ____________

Discussion Questions:

What existed before creation? ____________

How many days did it take to create everything? ____________

How did God create everything? ____________

What are some of the things God created? ____________

____

What does this story tell you about God, and how do you feel about Him for making all of these things?

____

____

Is there anyone more powerful than God? ____________

Questions I have: ____________

____

Activity of the day

CREATION	PLANTS
HEAVEN	SUN
EARTH	MOON
LIGHT	STARS
DARKNESS	NIGHT
WATER	DAY
LAND	SKY
CREATURES	MANKIND

```
I R Y K N G D P G D Y I U M X
U K G S U V A D N I G H T O S
S M I W E P R O H T R A E O P
Y K A N A L K R K R A D O N L
L I G O D T N S M A C I D T A
S U N I A E E A A N D A N H N
U J A T V S S R N D A G A F T
P L I A S N S R K G Y I L U S
R N E E P R I C I N I B C L T
U H O R A E A E N L I G H T N
I M Y C B D R T D U S R A E O
C R E A T U R E S L P L A M C
```

This week we are learning about...

Noah and the Ark

God was very disappointed in His people, and saw that they had become wicked. The Lord regretted making humans and He was deeply troubled by it. They were full of sin and destruction so God came up with a plan. He was going to send a flood to wipe out the human race and all the animals, but God found favor in a man named Noah. He was a faithful man and walked with God.

So God told Noah about His plans and told him to build an ark. God gave Noah specific plans on how to build it and told him to make it from cypress wood. It would have rooms inside and would be 350 cubits long, 50 cubits wide and 30 cubits high. There would be a door on the side of the ark and there would be lower, middle, and upper decks.

At this time the Lord told Noah that everything on the Earth was to perish but that when Noah and his family entered the ark they would be safe. Noah, his wife, his sons (Shem, Ham, and Japheth), and their wives were all invited to be on the ark. The Lord also instructed Noah that he was to bring seven pairs of clean animals and one pair of every unclean animal.

At the age of 600, Noah did everything just as God commanded him. When the floodwaters came, Noah and his family entered the ark along with all of the animals, and the rain fell on the earth for 40 days and 40 nights.

The water on the earth rose very high and all the dry land was covered. Even the mountains had more than 15 cubits of water over them. Every living thing on the land perished in the flood and the waters flooded the earth for 150 days.

God remembered Noah and sent a wind over the earth that caused the waters to recede. At the end of the 150 days the water had gone down. On the 17th day of the 7th month the ark came to rest on the mountains of Ararat. After 40 days Noah opened a window that he had made and sent out a raven to see if any land had dried up. He also sent out a dove, but the dove could not find anywhere to perch so it flew back to Noah. He waited 7 more days and sent the dove out again, this time when the dove returned in the evening it was holding a freshly plucked olive leaf. After another 7 days, Noah sent the dove out once again but this time it did not return.

Read through **Genesis 6-9:16**

By the 27th day of the 2nd month of Noah's 601st year of age, the Earth was completely dry. Then God commanded Noah and his family to come out of the ark along with all of the animals. Noah went and built an altar and had made burnt offerings to the Lord. That was pleasing to God Who said in His heart, "Never again will I curse the ground because of humans. And never again will I destroy all living creatures as I have done. As long as the Earth endures, seedtime and harvest, cold and heat, summer and winter, day and night will never cease."

"Whenever I bring clouds over the Earth and the rainbow appears in the clouds, I will remember my covenant between me and you and all living creatures of every kind. Never again will the waters become a flood to destroy all life. Whenever the rainbow appears in the clouds, I will see it and remember the everlasting covenant between God and all living creatures of every kind on the earth." – **Genesis 9:14-16, NIV** –

DAY ONE

Today's Date: ____________

Chapter Recap Questions:

Why did God send a flood upon the earth? ____________

____

Who did God find favor in, and who was on the ark? ____________

____

What type of wood was the ark made from? ____________

How old was Noah in the beginning and at the end of the story? ____________

How many days and nights did it rain for? ____________

How high over the mountains did the water rise? ____________

How many days did the waters flood the earth for? ____________

Where did the ark come to rest? ____________

What two types of birds did Noah send out? ____________

What did the bird return with? ____________

What appears in the clouds as a remembrance of God's covenant? ____________

Questions I have: ____________

____

DAY TWO

Today's Date: ____________

Yesterday we talked about how Noah walked with God. What would it be like to walk with God? Do we walk with God today?

Noah followed every one of Gods commands, would you have followed every step God told you to do? Why or why not?

In fact, this is
love for God:
to keep his commands.
And his commands are
not burdensome.

– 1 John 5:3, NIV –

Today's Prayer...

Need ideas? Try, I'm sorry for... I pray for... I praise You for...

What was the first thing Noah did when he got off the ark? Why did Noah do it?

The Lord then said to Noah, "Go into the ark, you and your whole family, because I have found you righteous in this generation." – **Genesis 7:1, NIV**

Activity of the day

Across

3. He was a faithful man who walked with God.
5. What did Noah build after he got off the ark?
7. Noah's first son.
8. Another name for the boat.
10. Measurement they used.
12. Brought back a freshly plucked olive leaf.
13. What did God send over the earth that caused the waters to recede?

Down

1. Book in the Bible in which the story took place.
2. Noah's third son.
4. Noah's second son.
6. Appears in the sky as a remembrance of God's covenant with us.
9. The first type of bird that Noah sent out.
11. What did God send to wipe out the human race?

DAY THREE

Today's Date: ______________

God blessed them and said, "Be fruitful
and increase in number and fill the water in the seas, and let
the birds increase on the earth." – Genesis 1:22, NIV

Questions/Notes I have:

Prayer of the day:

This week we are learning about...

The Tower of Babel

Did you know that the entire world once spoke the same language? As people started to multiply they eventually started moving East towards Shinar where they came to live.

One day the people came up with an idea. They were going to make bricks and use tar and build themselves a city. The city would have a tower that would be so tall it would reach up to heaven. The people wanted to make a city where they would all live so that they wouldn't be scattered over the whole earth.

When the Lord came to visit the city, He saw the tower they were building. God noticed that the people (who were speaking all the same language) thought they were powerful without God and had no limits. He scattered them all over the earth and gave them new languages so that they could no longer understand each other or continue building the city. It is known as Babel because the Lord confused their languages.

Read through
Genesis 11:1-9
In your Bible for the story.

DAY ONE

Today's Date: ____________

What were the people planning to do?

____

____

Why did God scatter them around the earth?

____

____

What has this story taught you?

____

____

____

Questions I have: ______________________

____

____

So the Lord scattered them from there over all the earth, and they stopped building the city. That is why it was called Babel—because there the Lord confused the language of the whole world. From there the Lord scattered them over the face of the whole earth.

– **Genesis 11:8-9, NIV**

My Presence
will go
with you,
And I will
give you rest
Exodus 33:14, NIV

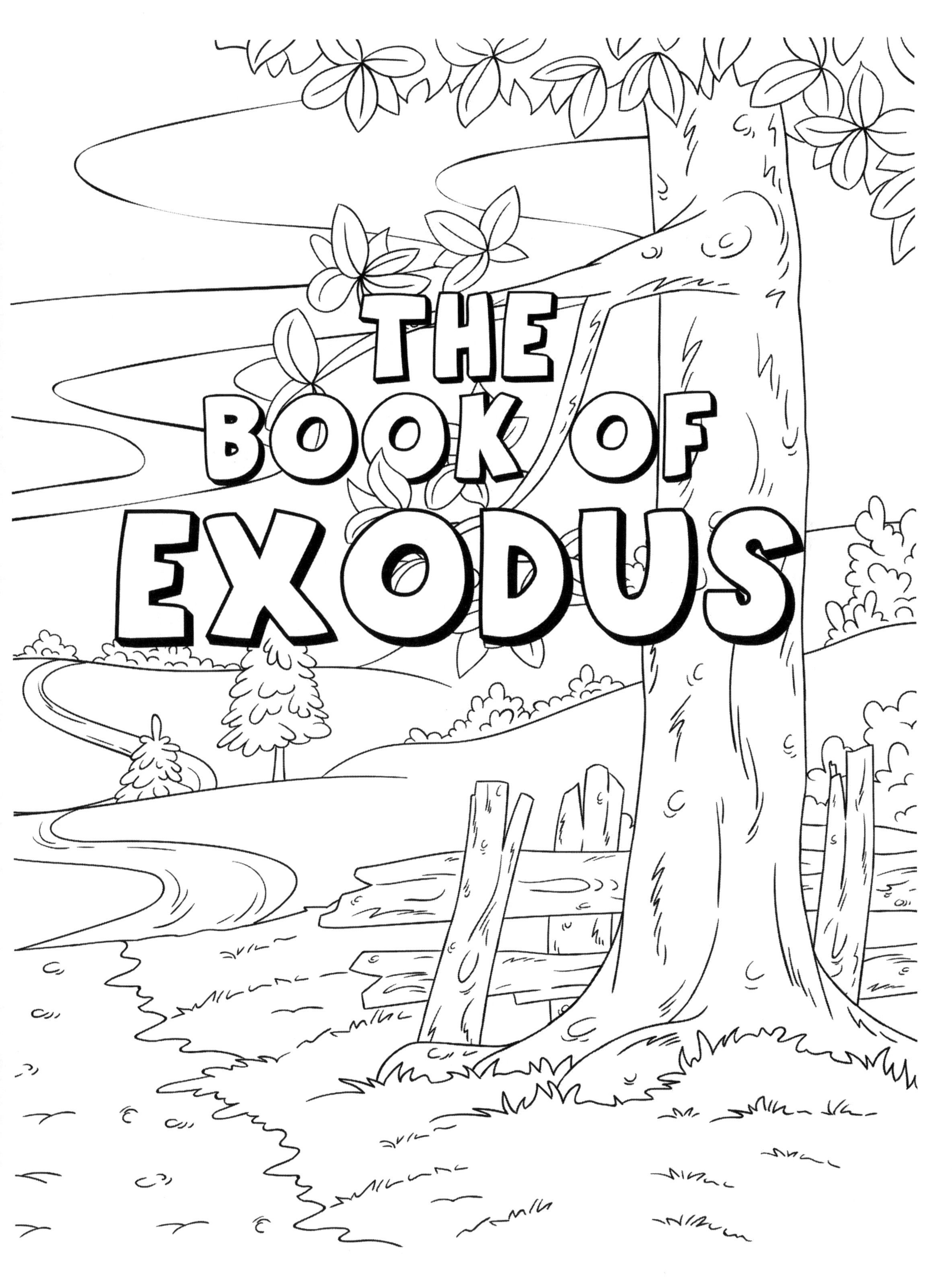
THE
BOOK OF
EXODUS

This week we are learning about...

The Birth of Moses

The Israelites had become extremely fruitful and blessed by God. They had multiplied and filled the land of Egypt. The story begins with a new king who had just come to power and was worried about how the Israelites were doing so well. The king was afraid that the Israelites had become too numerous and that they were starting to overpower his people so he appointed masters over them and forced them to be slaves.

After some time, the king noticed that even though he had set strict rules and made the Israelites slaves, they were still multiplying and spreading through Egypt. Their work had become harsher as the king started to worry more and more. The Egyptians worked them constantly keeping the Israelites busy.

Even though the work had become more intense, the Israelites still multiplied at large numbers. Shiphrah and Puah, the Hebrew midwives, were given instructions from the king. He instructed the women that while they were delivering babies, they would only be allowed to keep girls, and people were not allowed to have boys.

However, the women were God fearing and without telling the king, kept the girls and the boys. But the king soon found out and confronted them about it. The midwives answered the king and told him that the Hebrew women were not like the Egyptian women. They lied to the king and told him that the women were giving birth before they could make it in time.

God was pleased with how the midwives had stayed faithful to Him, and because they loved God and followed Him they were given families of their own and the people increased and became even more numerous. The king didn't like this and so he ordered every Hebrew boy to be thrown into the Nile river, but that every girl could live.

At this time, there was a man from the tribe of Levi. He had married a Levite woman and soon they were expecting a child together. When the couple saw their baby, they instantly fell in love with him and so the woman hid him for three months.

After a while, it became hard for her to hide him and so she got a basket and coated it with tar and pitch. The baby was put inside and the woman placed the basket in the reeds along the banks of the Nile river. The boy's sister stood by to see what would happen to him.

Just after the baby was placed in the river, the king's daughter had gone down to bathe in the Nile. Her and her attendants were walking along the riverbank when she saw the basket in the reeds and sent one of her female servants to get it. The king's daughter gently opened it and saw the small baby crying. She felt sorry for him and recognized that it was a Hebrew baby.

The baby's sister who was standing near the banks had gone over to the king's daughter and she asked her if she would like her to find a Hebrew woman to watch over and feed the baby for her. The daughter agreed and so the little girl went to find her mother.

The king's daughter told the boy's mom to take the baby and feed it for her and that she would be willing to pay. So, the boy's mom took him back and she was able to be with her son again. After he had grown older, the mom took the boy back to the king's daughter and he became her son. She named him Moses because she said "I drew him out of the water."

You can read through Exodus 1-2:1-10 in your Bible for the story

DAY ONE

Today's Date: ____________

Why did the new king dislike the Israelites?

____

____

Why did the king's daughter choose the name Moses?

____

____

Why was God pleased with the midwives?

____

____

Questions I have about the story of Moses: ____________________

____

Questions?

What are Israelites?
Descendants of Jacob are referred to as Israelites because in Genesis 32:27-28 Jacob's name was changed to "Israel".

What is a Pharaoh?
Both the word Pharaoh and king were used in this chapter but Pharaoh is the common title used for the monarchs of Ancient Egypt.

What is a Hebrew?
A Hebrew was typically referred to as a descendant of Abraham, Isaac, and Jacob who were introduced to us in Genesis.

Activity of the day

I	E	G	H	D	E	U	C	S	H	R	I	U	S	E
S	B	G	E	G	Y	P	T	I	M	V	I	L	H	B
M	A	Q	B	E	I	O	W	Z	Y	S	A	H	I	A
O	S	A	V	H	E	O	R	S	R	I	P	O	P	R
B	K	B	S	L	S	S	T	A	S	S	U	R	H	Y
A	E	K	W	E	R	B	E	H	W	D	A	G	R	G
A	T	O	S	P	K	L	E	G	D	H	L	W	A	E
I	N	O	V	E	I	A	N	R	S	R	A	Z	H	P
N	M	E	O	T	N	E	A	I	F	O	A	U	E	O
O	S	A	E	C	A	V	A	L	L	U	M	R	P	A
C	R	S	P	N	F	B	E	I	U	E	H	I	W	A

ISRAELITES BASKET PUAH EGYPT
SHIPHRAH HEBREW NILE MOSES

This week we are learning about...

Moses and the Burning Bush

Moses was out tending to his father-in-law's flock (Jethro, the priest of Midian) on the far side of the wilderness, when he came to Horeb, the mountain of God. While he was there, Moses noticed a bush on fire. The bush did not burn up in the flames and it stumped Moses, so he went to go see it. When God saw that Moses had gone to see the bush He called out to him.

God told Moses to take off his sandals, and to not come any closer than he was, because the place where he was standing was holy ground. Moses quickly hid his face because he was afraid to look at God.

The misery upon the people of Egypt had been going on too long and God heard them cry out to Him. They had become slaves and were suffering at the hands of the king. God explained to Moses that He had come down to rescue them from the Egyptians and bring them to a better land. One that He said would be a **"spacious land, a land flowing with milk and honey"** (Exodus 3:8B, NIV).

God saw how the Egyptians were treating the Israelites and He heard their cries. So God told Moses of His plans to free them. He said to Moses that he was to go to the Pharaoh in Egypt and demand that he let his people go.

Moses was unsure of the plan. **"Who am I that I should go to Pharaoh and bring the Israelites out of Egypt?"** (Exodus 3:11B, NIV) he asked. And God replied that He would be with Moses and told him that when he had brought the people out of Egypt that they would come back to the mountain and worship Him there.

"What will I tell them your name is if they were to ask?" Moses asked God. **"God said to Moses, "I am who I am. This is what you are to say to the Israelites: 'I am has sent me to you'"** (Exodus 3:15, NIV).

God instructed Moses to assemble the elders of Israel and tell them about the plan. He had told Moses that the elders would listen to him and that Moses would then take them to the king and say to him that they wanted to take a three-day journey into the wilderness to offer sacrifices to God. But God told Moses that He already knew the king of Egypt would not let them go so God would strike the Egyptians with wonders that only He could perform. After that, the king would let them go.

(The 10 plagues on Egypt is the next part of this story)

Read through Exodus 3:1-20 to see the full story in your Bible.

DAY ONE

Today's Date: ___________

Give a quick description of what the story is about in your own words.

God tells Moses that the pharaoh will not agree to his proposition to begin with but because of his stubbornness God will be able to show His power to every one in Egypt. Can you name another story where God shows off His amazing power?

The story of the burning bush is very important for the character of Moses. It is when he officially becomes a prophet. Later on in this book we'll see some of the other messages he has been given from God.

Down

1. Moses noticed a bush on _ _ _ _.
3. Moses came to Horeb, the _ _ _ _ _ _ _ _ of God.
4. Where God was going to free the Israelites from.
5. Moses had gone to see the _ _ _ _ then God called out to him.
6. Moses removed these when he was talking with God.
8. God heard the Israelites _ _ _ out to Him.

Across

2. God asked this man to go to the pharaoh in Egypt.
7. Another name for king, ruler over Egypt.
9. God instructed Moses to assemble the _ _ _ _ _ _ of Israel.

DID YOU KNOW? In Exodus 4:10, Moses pleaded with God asking Him if He could pick someone else to relay the messages because Moses wasn't a confident speaker.

This week we are learning about...

The Ten Plagues Of Egypt

In the previous story, we read about Moses and The Burning Bush. We learned about how God wanted Moses to go to Egypt to help free His people. This is the story of Moses talking with Pharaoh in Egypt and what God did in return to the Egyptians.

Moses was unsure that the Egyptians would believe him so God told him to throw the staff that was in his hand on the ground. When the staff hit the ground it immediately turned into a snake, and Moses ran from it. God told him to grab the snake by the tail, and so Moses reached out and it turned back into a staff. Then God told him to put his hand in his cloak and when Moses took it out his skin was leprous. And when God told him to put his hand back into his cloak, he listened: his hand returned to normal. The Lord told Moses that if the Egyptians did not believe that the Lord had sent him, then he should perform these acts in front of them, so they would believe him.

Moses was still hesitant and told the Lord that he was slow to speak and that He would be able to find someone more suitable for the job. **The Lord said to him, "Who gave human beings their mouths? Who makes them deaf or mute? Who gives them sight or makes them blind? Is it not I, the Lord?"** (Exodus 4:11, NIV). Then the Lord told Moses to go, and that He would help him speak. Moses again asked the Lord to send someone else. The Lord became angry and suggested Moses' brother Aaron to speak for him. God told Moses that He would help both of them to speak to the people. Aaron would give the messages from Moses that were given to him from God. So, Moses took his wife and sons, and went to Egypt on a donkey with the staff that God commanded him to take.

When Moses arrived in Egypt, he went to Pharaoh where he performed the wonders that God had given him the power to do. But God, hardened the heart of Pharaoh, so he would not let the people go.

Read through the next few days to see what God planned for Egypt, and how Pharaoh responded to God's command.

Read through Exodus 4 to see the full story in your Bible.

DAY ONE

Today's Date: ___________

THE TEN PLAGUES OVER EGYPT

Over the next few days we will be talking about the different wonders that God helped Moses perform in front of Pharaoh. We'll also talk about the ten plagues that God placed on Egypt. Here's a list of the ten plagues that we will be talking about --->

WATER TURNING INTO BLOOD, FROGS, GNATS, FLIES, SICK LIVESTOCK BOILS, HAIL, LOCUSTS, DARKNESS & DEATH OF FIRSTBORN CHILDREN

How do you think you would feel if God came to you asking you to talk to Pharaoh?

____

____

What were the two miracles that Moses performed?

____

____

____

How did Aaron become involved in the story?

____

____

QUESTIONS / NOTES: ___________

____

____

____

My Prayer of The Day ___________

____

____

____

DAY TWO

Today's Date: ___________

AARON'S STAFF BECOMES A SNAKE

You are the God who performs **MIRACLES**; you display your power among the peoples.

- Psalm 77:14, NIV -

Moses asked the Lord why He had brought him and Aaron to Egypt, because they were getting no results and the Israelites were treated worse than before. God's plan doesn't always make sense to us, but He knows more than we ever will and He can see the big picture while all we can see is the moment we're in. Even though it can be hard, we need to put our trust and faith into everything He decides for us.

The Lord gave a message to Moses to bring to the Israelites. He wanted them to know that He was going to free them from the Egyptians, and bring them to the land He swore to Abraham. But because of the rough conditions the Israelites were going through, they did not listen to Moses.

Now the Lord made Moses a powerful man in front of Pharaoh and Aaron, his brother. The Lord said once again to Moses that he was to ask Pharaoh to let His people go. God said He would harden Pharaoh's heart, and by it show signs and wonders to the people in Egypt. At this time Moses was eighty when he went to Pharaoh, and Aaron was eighty-three.

When Pharaoh asked for Moses to perform a miracle, God told Moses to say to Aaron to throw his staff on the ground before him and it would turn into a snake. So Moses and Aaron went before Pharaoh to do all that God had asked them to do. Pharaoh then summoned his wise men, sorcerers, and magicians together. They too were able to turn a staff into a snake for Pharaoh, but Aaron's staff swallowed up the magician's staff. Pharaoh's heart was not convinced and he would not listen to Moses and Aaron. He was evil, his slaves were valuable, and he did not want them to leave.

Seeing what Aaron and Moses could do, why didn't Pharaoh let the people go?

____

____

How old was Moses? How old was Aaron? ______________________

Why do you think God hardened the heart of Pharaoh?

____

____

So do not fear, for I am with you; do not be dismayed, for I am your God. I will strengthen you and help you; I will uphold you with my righteous right hand.
- Isaiah 41:10, NIV -

DAY THREE Today's Date: ____________

FIRST - WATER TURNING TO BLOOD

God could see that Pharaoh was going to take time to convince. He told Moses to go to him in the morning and approach him while he was at the Nile river. He then told Moses to take his staff with him.

Moses and Aaron went the next morning to see Pharaoh near the river. Again, they would do what God had told them to do. Aaron raised his staff in front of Pharaoh and his officials and he struck the water of the Nile. Immediately all of the water turned to blood, all the fish in the Nile died, and a strong foul smell filled Egypt. Because of this, the Egyptians were not able to drink any of the water.

Just as Pharaoh had done before, he gathered his magicians and they were able to perform the same acts and turn water into blood. Because of this, Pharaoh was not convinced, and he would not listen to Moses or Aaron. Since the water had turned to blood, the Egyptians were forced to dig around the river for their water.

Questions/Notes

____

____

____

____

____

____

____

____

What did Aaron and Moses do in front of Pharaoh?

____

____

____

Why do you think God started sending plagues to Egypt?

____

____

____

What did God tell Moses to take with them?

____

My Prayer of The Day

"I CAN DO ALL THIS THROUGH HIM WHO GIVES ME STRENGTH"

- Philippians 4:13, NIV -

Activity of the day

HAIL
AARON
BLOOD
STAFF
LOCUSTS
LICE
FLIES
FROGS
BOILS
MOSES
SNAKE
NILE
PHARAOH
LIVESTOCK

S	B	R	E	A	S	T	P	N	A	T	E	U	S	L
E	S	G	S	B	E	N	D	I	O	S	I	A	I	S
S	M	S	T	A	F	F	O	L	D	F	L	C	O	A
O	N	A	E	R	W	I	R	E	H	H	E	O	I	L
M	S	T	O	N	U	E	T	S	H	A	E	L	D	K
U	P	K	R	G	S	T	A	T	E	I	A	D	H	C
P	H	A	R	A	O	H	H	A	L	L	O	F	F	O
E	R	I	O	W	L	A	N	U	M	S	H	L	U	T
A	I	A	R	M	O	O	O	E	E	I	W	I	L	S
C	T	B	E	L	R	E	C	F	T	S	N	E	H	E
E	F	R	P	A	W	S	L	U	N	H	E	S	E	V
D	R	E	A	S	E	E	T	A	S	P	G	R	S	I
F	O	R	H	O	N	M	K	T	B	T	G	I	B	L
A	G	O	H	E	R	E	U	H	E	A	S	A	R	L
I	S	S	L	A	S	W	O	S	L	I	O	B	P	E
A	B	S	F	B	U	T	L	E	B	A	F	L	E	S

The story is Exodus 7:14-24 in your Bible.

DAY FOUR

Today's Date: ____________

SECOND – PLAGUE OF FROGS

It was seven days since the Lord turned the Egyptians' water to blood. The Lord told Moses to go back to Pharaoh and ask for him to let the Israelites go so that they could travel to the wilderness and worship God. He told Moses that if Pharaoh refused again, He would send another plague. This one would be frogs.

God told Moses to tell Aaron to stretch his hand over the Nile River with his staff. He would make frogs come out from the water. After Aaron stretched his hand over the water, the frogs came up and covered the land, filling the palace and Pharaoh's own bedroom. They occupied the houses of everyone in Egypt. They were everywhere.

Pharaoh quickly summoned Moses and Aaron and asked them to pray that the frogs would go away. In return, he would let the Israelites go. So Moses told Pharaoh that the frogs would be gone the next day and the plague would end.

When Moses left Pharaoh he prayed to God and asked Him to end the plague, and God answered. The frogs in all of the houses and fields died, and all of Egypt stunk. They were piled into heaps outside. When Pharaoh saw that the people were no longer suffering, his heart was again hardened and he decided that he would not let the people go.

Yesterday we talked about the first plague, water turning to blood.
How many days had it been since the first plague fell upon the Egyptians?

____

How did the second plague affect the Egyptians?

____

____

Did the Pharaoh end up agreeing to let the Israelites go? How did that turn out?

____

____

How long did this plague last? ______________________________

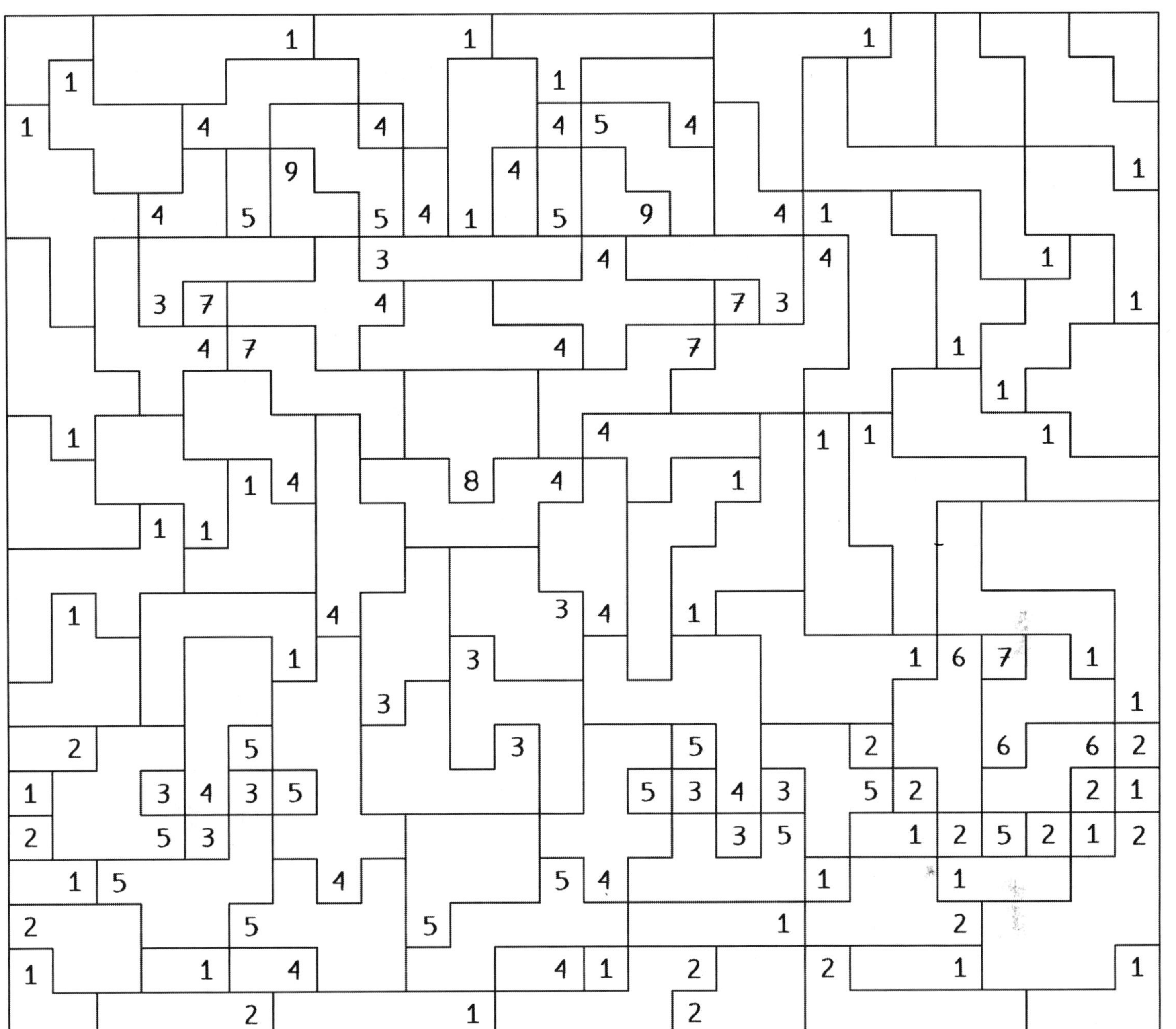

Questions And Notes

COLOR PUZZLE

Match up the color with the number on the puzzle above.

1. Light Blue
2. Dark Blue
3. Lime Green
4. Light Green
5. Dark Green
6. Yellow
7. Brown
8. Red
9. Black

The story is Exodus 7:25 - 8:15 in your Bible.

DAY FIVE

Today's Date: ______________

THIRD – PLAGUE OF GNATS

The Lord then told Moses to give Aaron a message. He was to stretch out his staff once again and strike the dust of Egypt and the dust would become gnats (small flying insects).

Aaron listened to God by striking the dust, causing the air to fill with gnats. They bothered the livestock and all of the Egyptians. Pharaoh summoned his magicians once again to see if they were able to perform the same acts but this time they could not.

Because the gnats were everywhere, the magicians told Pharaoh that it was the work of God. Pharaoh was so stubborn that he would not give up God's people.

The story is Exodus 8:16–19 in your Bible.

FOURTH – PLAGUE OF FLIES

Moses was told to get up early the next morning and confront Pharaoh as he was near the river. Moses asked Pharaoh once again if he would let the Israelites go and warned him that if he did not agree, the Lord would send swarms of flies to Egypt. Moses warned him that they would cover the ground and be in the Egyptians' houses and in the palace, but he also said that there would be no flies in the land of Goshen.

Goshen, where the Israelites lived, would be free from the plague so that the people could see the distinction between the Egyptians and God's people. He warned Pharaoh that the flies would come the next day and, just as he promised, they did. They poured into Pharaoh's palace and all the houses of the Egyptians, except for those in Goshen.

Pharaoh summoned Moses and Aaron and told them to offer their sacrifices to God in Egypt. Moses would not agree to the offer and said that they must take the three-day journey into the wilderness just as God had commanded them. Pharaoh agreed but told them he would only let the people go if they didn't go very far. He then asked Moses to pray for the plague to end. Moses agreed. When he left Pharaoh, Moses prayed for the Lord to end the plague, and by the next day not a single fly remained. As soon as they were gone, Pharaoh changed his mind once again.

The story is Exodus 8:20–32 in your Bible.

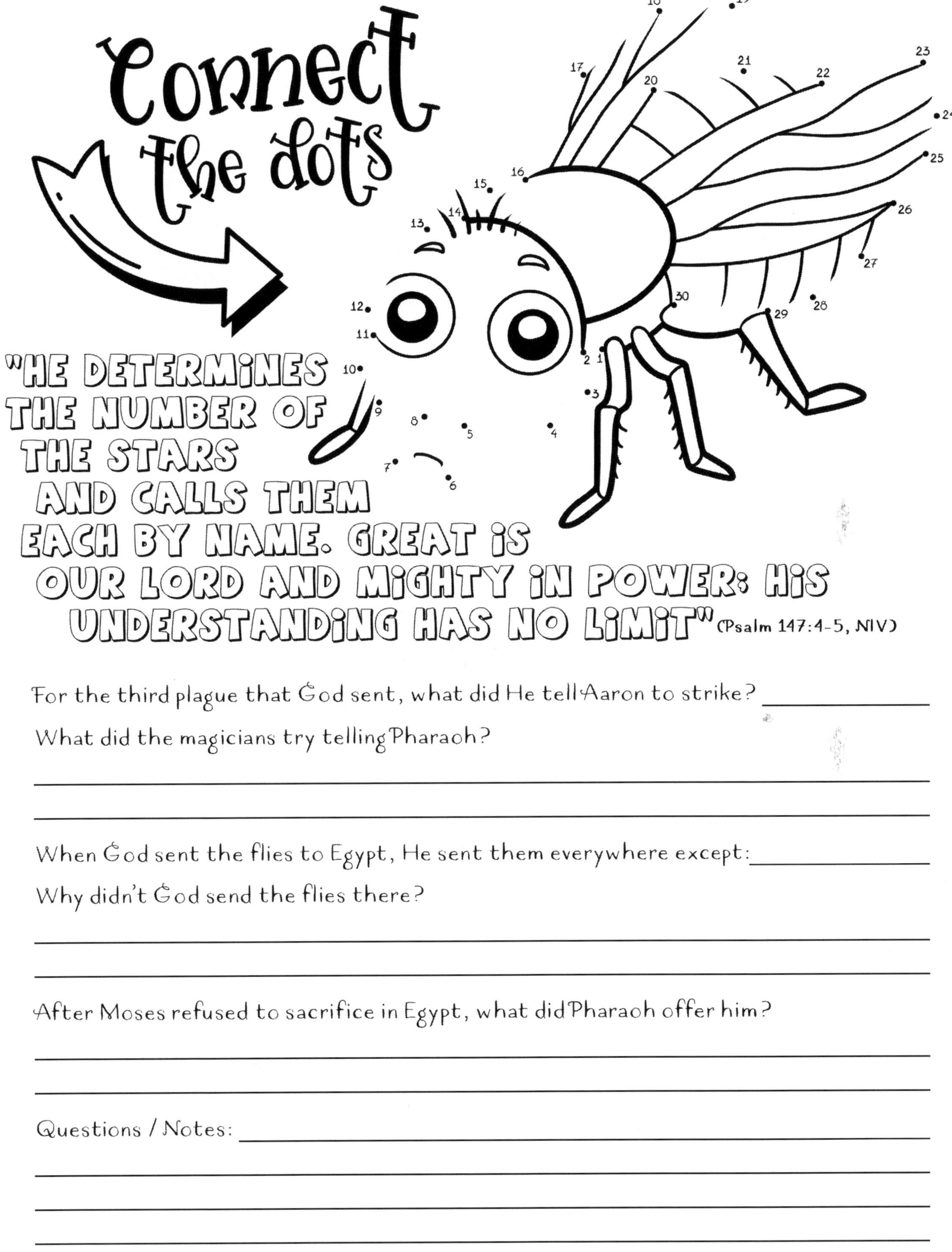

For the third plague that God sent, what did He tell Aaron to strike? ____________

What did the magicians try telling Pharaoh?

____

____

When God sent the flies to Egypt, He sent them everywhere except: ____________

Why didn't God send the flies there?

____

____

After Moses refused to sacrifice in Egypt, what did Pharaoh offer him?

____

____

Questions / Notes: ______________________________

____

____

____

DAY SIX

Today's Date: ____________

FIFTH – SICK LIVESTOCK

Then the Lord told Moses to go back to Pharaoh again so Moses did what God had asked and he warned Pharaoh about a terrible plague God was going to put on the livestock of all the Egyptian animals. Horses, donkeys, camels, sheep, cattle, and goats would all be affected. God also told Moses that the livestock of the Israelites would be safe and He would not put a plague on them.

The Lord had set a time for the next day when the plague would start.

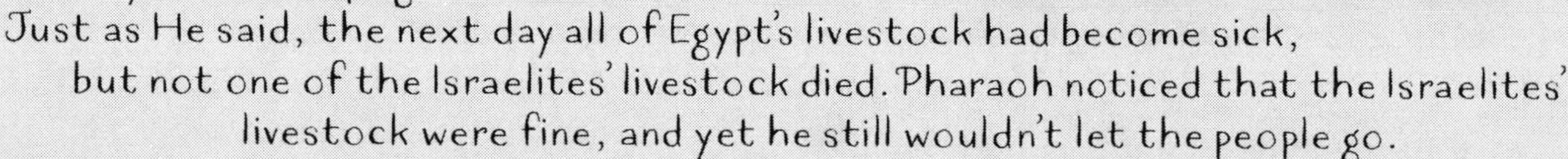

Just as He said, the next day all of Egypt's livestock had become sick, but not one of the Israelites' livestock died. Pharaoh noticed that the Israelites' livestock were fine, and yet he still wouldn't let the people go.

The story is Exodus 9:1–7 in your Bible.

When did the Lord say that He was going to put this plague on the Egyptians?

____

What did Pharaoh notice?

____

____

Why did God only put the plague on the Egyptians and not the Israelites?

____

My Prayer of The Day

____

____

____

Activity of The day

Can you figure out the Crossword?
We have made it half way through the story of the plagues. Let's take a look at what we've learned so far!

Down

1. Moses took his wife and sons, and went to Egypt on a ______ with the staff that God told him to take.

3. God turned the water to _____.

4. God sent 10 ______(s) to the Egyptians.

7. What Pharaoh asked Moses to do.

8. The name of God's people.

9. Fifth plague.

11. Turned into a snake.

13. Title of the ruler of Egypt

16. The amount of days that passed from the first plague to the second.

18. God turned the ____ into gnats.

Across

2. Second plague.

5. Fourth plague.

6. Spoke for Moses.

10. His staff turned into a _____.

12. People of Egypt.

14. These people told Pharaoh that the plagues were the work of God.

15. Aaron's brother.

17. Where the Israelites lived. Would be free from the plague.

19. Third plague.

DAY SEVEN Today's Date: ___________

SIXTH - THE PLAGUE OF BOILS

After Pharaoh had changed his mind once again, the Lord told Moses to take handfuls of soot from a furnace and toss it into the air. The soot would become fine dust over the entire land of Egypt and cause people and animals to break out in boils (red painful bumps that form under the skin).

Moses listened to God and he took soot from a furnace and tossed it into the air in front of Pharaoh. Everyone soon broke out with boils and the magicians were unable to see Moses because they too were covered in boils. But the Lord had hardened Pharaoh's heart once again and he would not listen to Moses and Aaron.

The story above is Exodus 9:8-12. The story below is Exodus 9:13-35.

SEVENTH - THE PLAGUE OF HAIL

God gave Moses instructions to get up early the next morning and go confront Pharaoh. Moses was instructed to give him a message from the Lord. He was to ask Pharaoh to let God's people go so that they could go and worship Him in the wilderness. God also had a warning for Pharaoh. If he didn't let the Israelites go, He would send His full force of plagues against them so that Pharaoh and all of the Egyptians would know that there was no other God like Him on Earth.

"For by now I could have stretched out my hand and struck you and your people with a plague that would have wiped you off the earth. But I have raised you up for this very purpose, that I might show you my power and that my name might be proclaimed in all the earth" (Exodus 9:15-16, NIV).

God warned Pharaoh that by the same time tomorrow He was going to send the worst hailstorm that Egypt had ever seen. He warned Pharaoh to tell the Egyptians to bring in all of their livestock and everything they had of value in from the fields. The officials who feared the Lord listened and they hurried to shelter everything they had. Some ignored the warning and left their livestock in the fields. As the Lord gave the command, Moses stretched out his hand toward the sky and hail fell over all of Egypt. Thunder, hail, and lightning filled the sky. It was by far the worst storm that anyone had ever seen. The storm raged on everywhere except for the land of Goshen.

Pharaoh summoned Moses and Aaron and said to them that he realized the Lord was in the right and his people were in the wrong. He asked for prayer over Egypt and gave permission for the people to go. But when Pharaoh saw that the storm had stopped, he sinned again and would not let the Israelites go.

What did God tell Moses to toss into the air? ______________________

Why were the magicians unable to see Moses? ______________________

What was God's warning to Pharaoh? ______________________

____

Why did God keep sending plagues on Egypt?

____

____

What did God say the Egyptians should do before the seventh plague started?

____

____

Who listened to the warning? ______________________

What did Pharaoh say when he summoned Moses and Aaron?

____

____

DAY EIGHT

Today's Date: ____________

EIGHTH – THE PLAGUE OF LOCUSTS

God told Moses that He had hardened the heart of Pharaoh and his officials so that He would be able to show His great signs among them. Moses and Aaron were sent back to Pharaoh once again and asked for him to let the people go or they would bring a plague of locusts to Egypt.

Moses warned Pharaoh, and when he left, Pharaoh's officials asked him how long he would keep the Israelites. They tried to change Pharaoh's mind and he ordered for Moses and Aaron to return. "Go, worship the Lord your God," he said to Moses, but asked in return that they would tell him who was going. **Moses answered, "We will go with our young and our old, with our sons and our daughters, and with our flocks and herds, because we are to celebrate a festival to the Lord"** (Exodus 10:9, NIV). Pharaoh refused and said that only the men could go. Then Moses and Aaron were driven out of the palace.

Moses stretched his hand over Egypt and caused an east wind to blow across the land. It brought the locusts which began to swarm, eating everything that was left in the fields and everything that grew on the trees. They covered the ground until it was black and nothing green remained on any tree or plant in all of Egypt.

Realizing what he had done, Pharaoh called for Moses and Aaron and asked for forgiveness. He asked them to pray that God would end the plague. God changed the direction of the wind, and carried the locusts away into the Red Sea. But, God hardened Pharaoh's heart and he still wouldn't let the people go.

What did Pharaoh's officials do?

____

Who/what did Moses say they were taking with them?

____

____

Who did Pharaoh say could go?

____

What damage did the locusts cause?

____

____

BUT I WILL HARDEN PHARAOH'S HEART, AND THOUGH I MULTIPLY MY SIGNS AND WONDERS IN EGYPT, HE WILL NOT LISTEN.
EXODUS 7:3-4

DAY NINE

Today's Date: ____________

NINTH - THE PLAGUE OF DARKNESS

Moses stretched his hand toward the sky and darkness covered Egypt for three days. People were unable to see each other or travel around but the Israelites had light where they lived. Pharaoh once again called for Moses and told him that the people could go worship God, but he insisted that they leave their livestock behind. Moses didn't agree with his proposition as they needed the livestock to offer sacrifices to God. Once again, God hardened the heart of Pharaoh so he would not let the people and the livestock go.

Pharaoh was angry and told Moses to leave. **Pharaoh said to Moses, "Get out of my sight! Make sure you do not appear before me again! The day you see my face you will die.""Just as you say," Moses replied. "I will never appear before you again." (Exodus 10:28-29, NIV)**

TENTH - THE PLAGUE ON FIRSTBORNS

The Lord told Moses that He was going to bring one more plague to Egypt. This one would surely cause Pharaoh to let His people go and Pharaoh would be forced to drive the Israelites out completely. Moses told the people what God had said. He warned them that by midnight God would go through Egypt and take the firstborn son of every person and animal. Pharaoh too would be affected by this plague. Crying would be heard throughout Egypt. But God told Moses that not a single person or animal would be taken from the Israelites if they obeyed God. By this, people would know that God was in control and watching His people.

These were the ten plagues that God performed in Egypt. We'll be talking a bit more about how God freed His people from Egypt in the next chapter.

Questions / Notes: ____

____

____

____

____

Activity of the day

HEBREW
PLAGUE
GOSHEN
ISRAELITES
HEART
SLAVERY
EGYPTIANS
GOD
MAGICIAN
RIVER

You can find the stories in
Exodus 10:21-29
Exodus 11
in your Bible.

H B R E I S R A E L I T E S L
E E M M B E N V I G S P L I S
S M A T A F F I L D O L C R A
O G A S R G I R E P H D O A L
M R I L N H I T S H L E L E K
N P O A G P E C T E T A S H C
E H G V A S L H I P L N G F O
H E H E B R E W Y A A H L U T
S L A R M T O G E I N W I L E
O T P Y R L E C T T S N E H E
G L R A A S S P U N H E S L V
D R E A S E Y T R E V I R S I
F H R A H G M K T B T G I B L
R G M H E E E U I S R G A R L
I S S L A S W O S R I O B P E

How long did darkness cover Egypt for?

Was there light anywhere?

When Pharaoh said he would let the people go, what was his one condition?

Who was safe from the tenth plague?

This week we are learning about...

The Ten Commandments

Do you know what The Ten Commandments are? The story takes place in the book of Exodus. God had freed the Israelites from slavery in Egypt and lead them to what would be the Promised Land. A land that God promised to Abraham's descendants.

As we read about in other chapters, God chose Moses to lead the people out of Egypt. Pharaoh was stubborn and wouldn't let them go. Eventually he did, and the people were free. As they wandered through the desert, God continued to give Moses instructions including The Ten Commandments.

On the first day of the third month after the Israelites had left Egypt, God brought them to the Desert of Sinai. They camped there in front of a mountain where Moses went up to talk with God. One day God told Moses to go back and tell the people to bathe and get ready, for He was going to appear and give them a message.

The Lord appeared as fire over the mountain and smoke filled the sky. The ground and the mountain trembled violently and the sounds of trumpets grew louder and louder in the air. The entire camp trembled and everyone knew that the Lord had come.

Moses had gone up the mountain to speak with the God but He told him to go back to the people and tell them not to follow him up or even touch the mountain. It was a special place where only Moses could go. Moses went down and told the people, then returned to God. He did not come back to the camp for 40 days and 40 nights.

God spoke to Moses about The Ten Commandments: rules that God made for his people to live by. Just like your parents have rules for you to live by, God does too. When God had finished speaking with Moses He gave him two tablets made from stone that were inscribed with these commandments:

1. Put God First
2. Have No Other Gods
3. Respect God's Name
4. Honor God's Day of Rest
5. Honor Your Parents
6. Do Not Kill
7. Honor Marriage
8. Do Not Steal
9. Do Not Lie
10. Do Not Be Jealous

DAY ONE

Today's Date: ______________

FIRST – PUT GOD FIRST

The Ten Commandments are a set of very important rules that we as Christians need to follow. The first of which is to put God first. In the Bible it is written as **"You shall have no other gods before me"** (Exodus 20:3, NIV). In our lives we must always put God first. He is the most important relationship we will ever have.

Do you have any idea how to do this? Maybe you can start off your day with prayer, volunteer at your church, commit to reading more Christian books, read your Bible, or even journal your faith. All of these are good ways to connect you with God.

Trust in the Lord with all your heart and lean not on your own understanding; in all your ways submit to him, and he will make your paths straight.
PROVERBS 3:5-6, NIV

My PRAYER of the day

Need ideas? Try thanking God for His unfailing love

____
____
____
____
____
____
____

What are some ways that you have been putting God first in your life?

____
____
____
____

What is one new way you will start putting God first in your life?

____
____
____
____

Questions I have about the story and the 1st commandment.

____
____
____
____

DAY TWO

Today's Date: ____________

SECOND – NO OTHER GODS

The second commandment that God gives to his people is **"You shall not make for yourself an image in the form of anything in heaven above or on the earth beneath or in the waters below. You shall not bow down to them or worship them"** (Exodus 20:4-5, NIV).

God asks us not to worship anything more than we worship Him. Nothing on Earth could ever compare to God. The Lord also says in this commandment that we should not make any images or statues of other false gods for we should only worship Him. We need God in our life.

Did you know?

While Moses was on the mountain talking with God, the Israelites gave up hope because Moses was taking so long to come back. Aaron told the people to gather their gold and they made a statue of a calf that they worshiped.

Read through Daniel 3:1-30 in your Bible.

Describe the image the King made.

____

____

____

What were all the people told to do when they heard the sound of the horn?

____

____

The name of the three men 1. __________ 2. __________ 3. __________

What happened to the men when they were thrown into the furnace?

____

____

Can you name any modern day idols? (Maybe you can ask your parents to help you think of some)

____

Questions I have about the second commandment / story.

____

My Prayer of the Day

Need ideas? Thank Him for something you're grateful for.

DAY THREE Today's Date: ____________

THIRD – HONOR GOD'S NAME

The Bible tells us **"You shall not misuse the name of the Lord your God, for the Lord will not hold anyone guiltless who misuses his name"** (Exodus 20:7, NIV).

Would you ever say anything rude against your best friend? Probably not, because you respect them and care for them. The Lord is very special and it is rude to disrespect His name. We need to be careful with how we use it and we cannot use it carelessly or to be rude towards other people. Keep in mind what you're saying and only say the best about God.

Salvation is found in no one else, for there is no other name under heaven given to mankind by which we must be saved

ACTS 4:12, NIV

Did you know that God has multiple different names? What are some names you use for God?

___

Have you ever misused the name of the Lord? Did you ask for His forgiveness?

___

___

Will everyone some day honor the name of God? (Read Psalm 145)

___

___

Questions I have: ___

___

___

My Prayer of The Day

___

___

___

___

Activity of the day

Use the alphabet below to unlock the verses.

1 3 4 5 A B C D E F

G H I J K L M N O

P Q R S T U V W X Y Z

CAN YOU FIGURE OUT WHAT THE SECRET VERSES ARE?

DAY FOUR

Today's Date: ____________

FOURTH – RESPECT GOD'S DAY OF REST

The fourth commandment that God gives to His people is **"Remember the Sabbath day by keeping it holy"** (Exodus 20:8, NIV).

God created the world in six days. On the seventh day He rested. Keeping the Sabbath day is important to God because it is a day He wants us to rest and focus on Him. On the Sabbath day (this might be Sunday for you), you and your family should take a day to relax, focus on God, and enjoy the blessings He has given to you.

Why does God want us to keep a Sabbath day?

____

____

What are you supposed to do on the Sabbath day? You can look up Leviticus 23:3.

____

____

Questions I have about the fourth commandment.

____

____

____

My Prayer of The Day

____

____

____

____

Observe the Sabbath day by keeping it holy, as the Lord your God has commanded you. Six days you shall labor and do all your work, but the seventh day is a sabbath to the Lord your God. On it you shall not do any work, neither you, nor your son or daughter, nor your male or female servant, nor your ox, your donkey or any of your animals, nor any foreigner residing in your towns, so that your male and female servants may rest, as you do. Remember that you were slaves in Egypt and that the Lord your God brought you out of there with a mighty hand and an outstretched arm. Therefore the Lord your God has commanded you to observe the Sabbath day. **(Deuteronomy 5:12-15, NIV)**

Activity of the day

Down

1. You need to _______ God's name.

4. Do not ______.

6. God had brought the Israelites to the Desert of _____.

7. Do not be ________.

9. The man who visited with God on the mountain.

12. Put ___ first.

13. No ____ gods.

15. What book of the Bible does this story take place in?

16. The form God appeared as over the mountain.

17. How many days and nights Moses was on the mountain for.

Across

2. Respect your _______.

3. Do not ___.

5. God gave Moses two stone _______.

8. Honor _________.

10. Do not ____.

11. Honor God's day of ____.

14. God gave us ten rules which we call the ten _____________.

18. The sounds of ________ grew louder and louder in the air.

ALL THE ANSWERS CAN BE FOUND IN THIS BOOK

(TEN COMMANDMENTS CHAPTER)

1 2 3 4 5 6 7 8 9 10 11 12 13 14 15 16 17 18

DAY FIVE

Today's Date: ____________

FIFTH – HONOR YOUR PARENTS

Have you ever done anything to disrespect your parents? Maybe you lied to them when they asked you if you did something, or maybe you spoke back to one of them. The Bible tells us to honor our father and mother and to respect them. Just like we are to respect God and to be kind to Him, we are also to be kind to our parents.

Read through **EPHESIANS 6:1-4** in your Bible.

Why is it important that we honor our parents?

____

____

____

____

Do you think adults have to respect and honor their parents? Why / Why not?

____

____

What are ways you show your parents respect?

____

____

____

Questions I have: ____________

____

____

My Prayer of The Day

Need ideas? Pray for a happy family, a good day, and for God to give you ideas on how to show respect to your parents.

____

____

____

HONOR YOUR
PARENTS

DAY SIX

Today's Date: ____________

SIXTH – DO NOT KILL

In Exodus, the Lord tells us **"You shall not murder"** (Exodus 20:13, NIV).

Do you remember the story of Cain and Abel? Cain was the firstborn son of Adam and Eve. Cain and his brother Abel both made offerings to the Lord but God preferred Abel's offering and it made Cain very jealous. Cain murdered Abel because of it and it made the Lord very sad.

God made us all unique and precious. Life is a very valuable thing and it upsets God when we turn against other people. As Christians, we cannot think the same way Cain did and still be close with God. To be close with God is to be filled with love.

Read through **GENESIS 4:1-16** in your Bible.

How does it make God feel when we break a commandment?

____

____

Who were Cain and Abel? What jobs did they each have?

____

____

What kind of offerings did each brother present to God?

____

____

Why do you think Cain's offering wasn't accepted?

____

____

Why did Cain kill his brother?

____

____

Questions I have: ______________________________

____

My Prayer of The Day

Activity of The day

Ten Commandments
scripture match up
(You can look all of these up in your Bible)

Draw a line between the verse and the commandment

1. "You shall not misuse the name of the Lord your God"	First commandment
2. "Honor your father and your mother"	Second commandment
3. "You shall not commit adultery"	Third commandment
4. "You shall not make for yourself an image in the form of anything in heaven"	Fourth commandment
5. "You shall not murder"	Fifth commandment
6. "You shall not covet your neighbor's house"	Sixth commandment
7. "You shall have no other Gods before me"	Seventh commandment
8. "You shall not give false testimony against your neighbor"	Eighth commandment
9. "Remember the Sabbath day by keeping it holy"	Ninth commandment
10. "You shall not steal"	Tenth commandment

DAY SEVEN

Today's Date: ____________

SEVEN – HONOR MARRIAGE

In the seventh commandment God says, **"you shall not commit adultery"** (Exodus 20:14, NIV). What does this mean? In simple terms, it means respect and honor marriage. A married couple should stay faithful to their promises and shouldn't betray each other. Marriage is a promise to God that you both will stay faithful and stand by each other. To break that vow would be to break a promise with your spouse, and also with God.

Genesis says **"a man leaves his father and mother and is united to his wife, and they become one flesh"** (Genesis 2:24, NIV). Although this commandment talks about marriage it still applies to everyone. Even though you might not be married you need to respect the rules of marriage. Satan has made people believe that sinful thoughts and actions are okay, but even a little bit is like a drop of poison in a drink. It's not safe. God made marriage a very special bond, not only between a husband and wife but also with God.

Read through GENESIS 2:19-24

Why is it important to God that we respect marriage?

____

____

What does marriage mean to you?

____

____

How and why did God create Eve?

____

____

My Prayer of The Day ______________________________

____

____

____

HONOR
MARRiAGE

DAY EIGHT

Today's Date: ____________

EIGHTH – DO NOT STEAL

Read through GENESIS 27:1–41 in your Bible. We are going to be talking about the story of the blessing over Jacob and Esau.

Stealing is a very bad sin to commit. The Bible tells us that we **"shall not steal"** (Exodus 20:15, NIV) and yet it is very common for people to do.

God provides everything that we need and we should be thankful for what we have. Sometimes adults and kids can be tempted to take things that is not theirs. God tells us not to steal. Instead we should be focused on helping others and giving to them.

Why does God say it's wrong to steal? Is it ever alright to steal?

What did Jacob steal? Why do you think he did it?

Was it ok to do what Jacob did?

How many, and what types of commandments did Jacob break?

Are there other examples of stealing that you can think of?

Questions I have:

EPHESIANS 4:28, NIV Anyone who has been stealing must steal no longer, but must work, doing something useful with their own hands, that they may have something to share with those in need.

Activity of the day

MOUNTAIN EXODUS
ISRAELITES LIE
MOSES STEAL
GOD FIRE
SMOKE IDOLS
TRUMPETS SABBATH
PARENTS MURDER
MARRIAGE JEALOUS
COMMANDMENTS
DESERT OF SINAI

D B G O A S A B B A T H U S Q
H E G S T E N S C O S I A I S
S X S T E M G T J G M L D S A
T T A E O W S E E H O I O R P
R R N M R U E A A H K E L A V
U U I E D T T L L I E A R E J
P M O O M S O H O S S E I L T
E P X S W D A F U M N H E I I
F E A R I O N O S T R W M T N
I T E I L N E A S I R S D E I
E S R D R W S S M U N E I S A
M U R D E R L T S M D A R S T
F F R H O O L E T B O G I P N
S I P R D E S U U E G C A A U
M R S I J O W L I M N A S P O
A E X F M A R R I A G E L E M

What I'm praying for today...

Need ideas? Try praying for those who need guidance, or thanking the Lord for something He's done in your life.

The thief comes only to steal and kill and destroy; I have come that they may have life, and have it to the full.

- John 10:10, NIV -

DAY NINE

Today's Date: ______________

NINTH – DO NOT LIE

Read through **GENESIS 3** in your Bible.

When the Bible says **"You shall not give false testimony against your neighbor"** (Exodus 20:16, NIV), it is telling us not to lie. It can seem easy to lie.

Sometimes we do it to get out of trouble, and sometimes we do it so that we get what we want. Lying, even though it doesn't seem like it, will always have bad results. God wants us to speak truthfully to each other and to always be honest.

Why is lying a bad thing?

____

____

Is any lie alright to tell, even if it's only a small lie?

____

____

Who can you name in the Bible that lied?

____

____

What did Adam and Eve do?

____

____

Do you think God knew what they had done before they told Him?

____

____

What were the consequences of their actions?

____

____

Questions I have: ______________________________

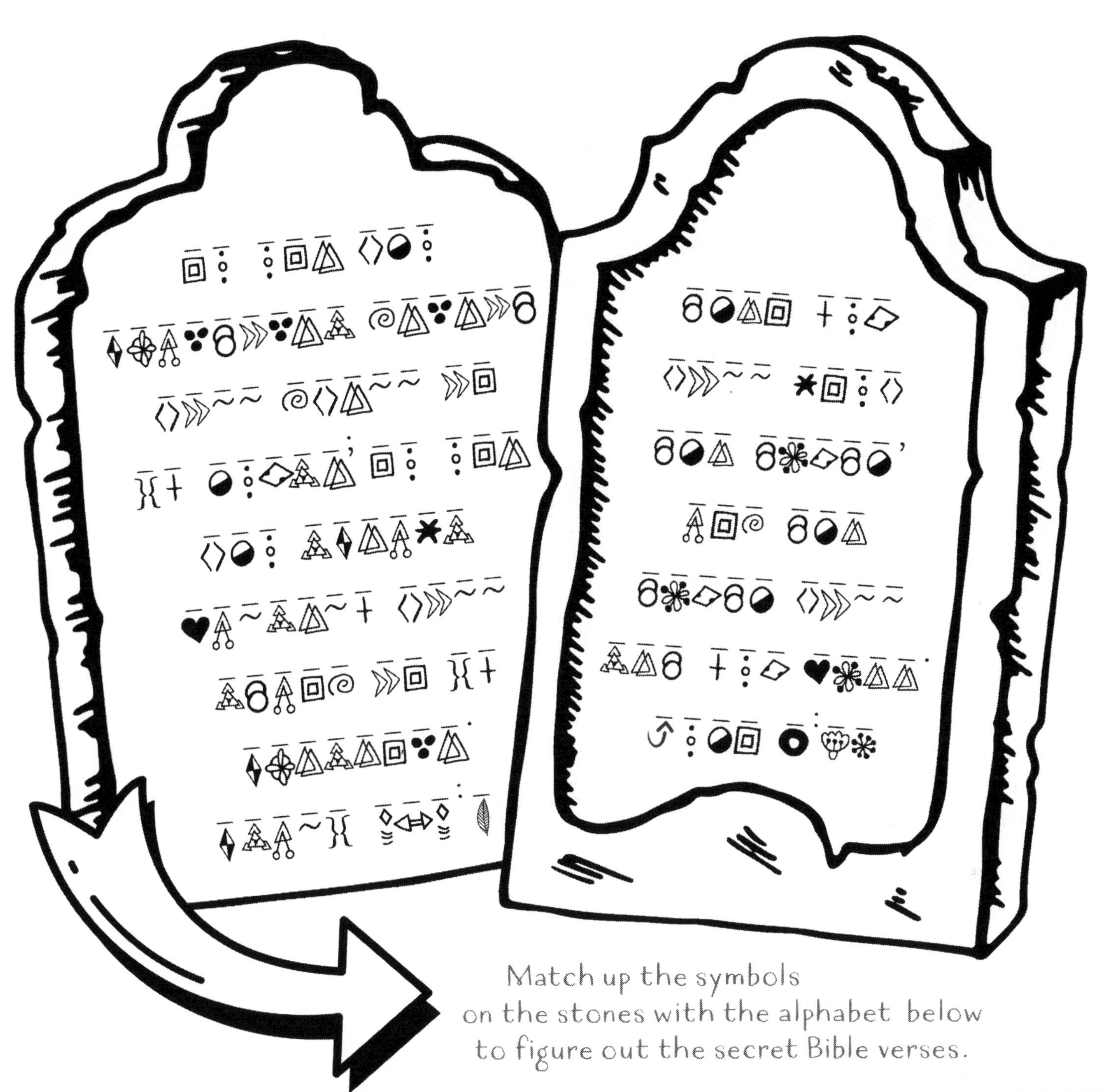

Match up the symbols on the stones with the alphabet below to figure out the secret Bible verses.

CAN YOU FIGURE OUT WHAT THE SECRET VERSES ARE?

0 1 2 3 4 5 6 7 8 9

A B C D E F G H I J K

L M N O P Q R S T U V W X Y Z

DAY TEN

Today's Date: ____________

TENTH - DO NOT BE JEALOUS

Read through **GENESIS 37** in your Bible.

Have you ever been jealous of something someone else had? Maybe it was a new toy or maybe they got to do something you couldn't. Jealousy is the tenth sin that God lists.

Satan wants us to focus on what we can't have. He wants us to be jealous and unhappy, while God wants us to focus on what we do have. He has given us everything that we need.

When we look back at all of the commandments we can see that God just wants us to be truly happy. He has set these rules so that we can separate ourselves from Satan and so that we can live Christ-filled lives.

Why did Israel love Joseph more than his other sons? What gift did he give to him?

____

____

Originally, what did Joseph's brothers plan to do to him?

____

____

What did they change their plans to? Whose idea was it?

____

____

____

What did the brothers tell their father when they returned?

____

____

What types of things have you been jealous about?

____

____

Questions I have: ______________________________

____

LOVE
DISCIPLES
OBEDIENCE
HEART
COVENANT
PSALM 119:2, NIV
Blessed are those who keep his statutes and seek him with all their ________.
PSALM 128:1, NIV
Blessed are all who fear the Lord, who walk in ________ to him.
1 JOHN 4:16, NIV
And so we know and rely on the ________ God has for us. God is love. Whoever lives in love lives in God, and God in them.
JOHN 13:34-35, NIV
A new command I give you: Love one another. As I have loved you, so you must love one another. By this everyone will know that you are my ________, if you love one another.
DEUTERONOMY 4:13, NIV
He declared to you his ________ the Ten Commandments, which he commanded you to follow and then wrote them on two stone tablets.
CAN YOU HELP THE ANTS GET THEIR MISSING WORDS TO THE PROPER BIBLE VERSE?

And who knows but
that you have come to your
ROYAL POSITION
for such a time as this? 

– Esther 4:14, NIV –

THE BOOK OF ESTHER

This week we are learning about...

Esther Part 1 - Queen Vashti

At the time King Ahasuerus was ruler over the ancient city of Susa, located in the lower Zagros Mountains.

(In the NIV Bible they refer to him as King Xerxes but he is most commonly known as King Ahasuerus.)

It was in the third year of his reign when he decided to throw a large banquet. He had all of his nobles, officials, military leaders, and princes at the banquet where he showed off his wealth and kingdom for one hundred and eighty days.

After the one hundred and eighty days, the king threw another party. This time it was for everyone in the kingdom and it was held in the private garden at the palace. The poor and rich all gathered together for seven days as wine was served to everyone in gold cups, all different from one another, by the King's command. During this time, Queen Vashti was also throwing a banquet of her own. This one was only for the women.

On the seventh day, when King Ahasuerus had been drinking, he asked the men who served him to bring in Queen Vashti. He wanted to display her beauty in front of all the people at the banquet but she refused to come and this made the King very angry.

King Ahasuerus discussed the manner with his wise men which was a common thing for a king to do during those times. Kings would often discuss matters of the law with their wise men. Because the Queen had not obeyed the King and had not obeyed the law, King Ahasuerus issued a royal decree stating that Queen Vashti was to never enter the presence of the King again. He had also decided that her royal position would be given to someone else.

Then, when the King had time to think about it and his anger had subsided, the King's personal attendants proposed, "Let a search be made for beautiful young virgins for the King. Let the King appoint commissioners in every province of his realm to bring all these beautiful young women into the harem at the citadel of Susa. Let them be placed under the care of Hegai, the King's eunuch, who is in charge of the women; and let beauty treatments be given to them. Then let the young woman who pleases the King be queen instead of Vashti." This advice appealed to the King, and he followed it.

- Esther 2:2-4, NIV -

You can read through Esther 1-2:4 in your Bible for part 1

DAY ONE

Today's Date: ______________

What did Queen Vashti do to upset the King?

____

____

What did the King take away from Queen Vashti?

____

____

Prayer of the day

Need ideas? Maybe someone in your family is in need of prayer, or a friend at school or church.

____

____

____

____

____

____

The King and his wise men found Queen Vashti's actions to be very disrespectful as a wife. The men were worried that if she wasn't punished then other women in the kingdom would hear about what she did and would act disrespectful towards their own husbands.

Questions / Notes:

____

____

____

____

____

Esther chapter one is the lead up to the story of Esther that we will start talking about tomorrow. Without King Ahasuerus taking away Queen Vashti's crown and royal position there wouldn't be the story of Esther.

This week we are learning about...

Part 2 - Esther Made Queen

"Now there was in the citadel of Susa a Jew of the tribe of Benjamin, named Mordecai son of Jair, the son of Shimei, the son of Kish, who had been carried into exile from Jerusalem by Nebuchadnezzar king of Babylon, among those taken captive with Jehoiachin king of Judah." (Esther 2:5-6, NIV)

Mordecai had a cousin named Hadassah, also known as Esther, whom he had raised because she was an orphan. Esther was a beautiful young woman and when she heard about the King's order, she along with many young women were all taken to the palace and entrusted to Hegai but Mordecai gave her strict instructions before going to the palace. No one was to know her nationality or family background. Mordecai had forbidden her to tell anyone, because he didn't think she had a fair chance of being queen if they knew she was a Jew.

Immediately she won Hegai's favor and he provided her with all of her beauty treatments and special foods. He had even assigned seven female attendants from the King's palace to Esther and moved them to the best place in the harem. Every day Mordecai walked back and forth near the courtyard of the harem to find out how Esther was doing.

During this time, it was customary for a young woman to complete twelve months of beauty treatments, six months with oil of myrrh, and six with perfumes and cosmetics. They could take whatever they wanted with them from the harem to the King's palace. A woman was not allowed to return to the King unless she was invited by him.

When it came time for Esther to meet the King, she took the advice from Hegai, the King's eunuch who was in charge of the harem, and asked for nothing more than he suggested. Everyone that saw Esther loved her. She won over the favor of everyone at the palace. During the seventh year of King Ahasuerus' reign Esther was brought to him to meet her. He was immediately attracted to her, more than any other woman that he had met. The King chose Esther and he set a royal crown on her head and made her queen instead of Vashti. A great and large banquet was thrown in honor of Esther for all of the King's nobles and officials.

You can read through Esther 2:1-18 in your Bible for part 2

Questions / Notes: ______________________________

____

DAY TWO

Today's Date: ______________

Why do you think Mordecai didn't want anyone to know Esther's background?

____

____

____

How many years had passed since the first chapter?
(You can read through part 1 and 2 again for clues)

____

What was the relationship between Esther and Mordecai? How were they related?

____

____

A	M	O	R	D	E	C	A	I	D	I	G	X	F	R
O	I	P	Y	X	M	E	R	E	H	E	H	Z	O	R
R	E	E	A	E	E	A	C	E	E	A	E	Y	L	P
H	J	U	G	R	E	X	K	T	S	P	A	R	N	A
E	K	N	P	X	G	R	L	S	T	L	H	N	E	L
G	V	U	R	E	A	N	A	R	H	P	Y	W	S	A
A	G	C	R	S	O	D	I	I	E	A	H	O	S	C
I	X	H	U	R	A	D	U	K	R	A	K	R	J	E
V	A	S	S	H	L	M	R	S	T	J	O	C	P	E
J	E	W	C	R	I	T	H	S	A	V	F	L	X	S

Activity of the day:

FIND THE MISSING WORDS IN THE WORD SEARCH

ESTHER SUSA HAREM ROYAL
KING MORDECAI EUNUCH VASHTI JEW
HEGAI HADASSAH XERXES PALACE CROWN

Questions?

Who was Hegai?
He was a eunuch placed in charge of the harem.

What is a harem?
It was the private space for the women to stay, or the group of women who stayed there.

What is a eunuch?
A special guard trained to protect the women's living areas. A man who is fully trusted to focus on his job without being distracted by the beautiful women. Kings would be able to trust these men with their queens, princesses and their attendants.

What happens if you see the king without being invited?
"All the king's officials and the people of the royal provinces know that for any man or woman who approaches the king in the inner court without being summoned the king has but one law: that they be put to death unless the king extends the gold scepter to them and spares their lives."
(Esther 4:11, NIV)

This week we are learning about...

Part 3 - Haman and the Jews

After Esther had become queen she was still keeping her family and nationality a secret. One day the women were all asked to assemble for a second time. When Mordecai was sitting at the gate entrance to the palace, he overheard two of the guards who were guarding the doorway. The two men, Bigthana and Teresh, were overheard conspiring a plan to assassinate the king.

Mordecai, still unknown to be Esther's cousin, told Esther who reported the men to the King. The report was found to be true and the two officers were punished and impaled on poles. Esther told the King that Mordecai was the one to tell her about the plot and Mordecai was given credit from the King for reporting the men.

Not long after, the King appointed a new chief minister named Haman. His title was higher than all the nobles, and so the King commanded that everyone was to pay honor to him and kneel down in his presence, but Mordecai would not kneel down or pay him any honor. Mordecai despised him because Haman was a descendant of king Agog, an Amalekite. (The Amalekites has been enemies of the Jewish people for years).

The royal officials asked Mordecai why he wouldn't obey the King, but he still refused to kneel to Haman. The officials went to Haman and told them that Mordecai was not respecting the King's wishes and that he was a Jew. Haman was furious that Mordecai wouldn't kneel down to him. Having learned who he was, Haman decided to punish him, but instead of just punishing Mordecai, Haman decided that he was going to kill all of the Jews in the kingdom.

In the twelfth year of King Ahasuerus' reign a lot was cast (like rolling dice) in the presence of Haman to select a day for the punishment. The lot ended up falling on the twelfth month. Haman had told the king that the Jew's customs were different from everyone else's and that they did not obey the king's laws. Haman suggested that a decree should be issued to destroy them, and that he in return would give ten thousand talents of silver to the King's administrators for the royal treasury. The King agreed and took his signet ring from his finger and gave it to Haman but told him to keep his money.

The royal secretaries were then summoned and wrote out the orders that Haman had made. The orders were sent out to all the King's provinces stating that all Jews, young and old, women and children, were to be killed on the thirteenth day of the twelfth month. The orders were issued to every province and made a law that everyone would be ready for that day.

You can read through Esther 2:19-23 and Esther 3 in your Bible for part 3

DAY THREE Today's Date: ____________

NOTES / QUESTIONS: ____________

____

____

____

Activity of the day

Today we are going to be taking a break from the questions and jump into some Bible trivia! Match up the name of the person you think the sentence applies to. Answers can be found in days 1, 2, and 3 of this book.

1. ________ Heard the two guards plotting to kill the king.
2. ________ Also known as Esther.
3. ________ Descendant of King Agog, an Amalekite.
4. ________ Forbid Esther from telling anyone she was a Jew.
5. ________ Chosen by the king to be queen.
6. ___&___ Punished for plotting to kill the king.
7. ________ Would not kneel down towards the chief minister.
8. ________ Refused to go to the king.
9. ________ Jew from the tribe of Benjamin.
10. ________ The king's eunuch who was in charge of the harem.
11. ________ The king issued a royal decree stating that this person would never be able to enter the presence of the King again.
12. ________ Decided to punish all Jews in the kingdom.
13. ________ King during this time.

Names to match up:

(And yes, they can be reused)

A - Vashti
B - Hadassah
C - Mordecai
D - Hegai
E - Teresh
F - Ahasuerus
G - Esther
H - Bigthana
I - Haman

This week we are learning about...

Part 4 - Mordecai Asks for Help

The news of Haman's order quickly spread throughout the kingdom. As soon as Mordecai heard what Haman had done, he tore off his clothes and replaced them with sackcloth and ashes. Other Jews did the same, and they also started fasting. Mordecai walked through the city crying loudly until he came to the King's gate.

When Esther heard about Mordecai mourning outside of the palace she was very sad. She tried sending clothes for him, but Mordecai would not accept them. So, Esther ordered Hathak, one of the King's eunuchs, to find out what was troubling Mordecai. (It was a rule that no one dressed in sackcloth was allowed to enter the palace.)

Mordecai explained everything to Hathak that had happened. He also gave him a copy of the order that had been published in Susa so that Esther could read it, and asked that Esther go to the king to beg for mercy for the Jewish people.

The news of what Mordecai said was reported back to Esther. She instructed Hathak once again to go back to him and tell him that the king hadn't asked for her for thirty days. Any man or woman that approached the king without an invitation could be put to death unless he extended his gold scepter to them to spare their lives.

When Hathak told Mordecai what Esther had said,

He sent back this answer: "Do not think that because you are in the king's house you alone of all the Jews will escape. For if you remain silent at this time, relief and deliverance for the Jews will arise from another place, but you and your father's family will perish. And who knows but that you have come to your royal position for such a time as this?"

(Esther 4:13-14, NIV)

So Esther sent one last message to Mordecai. She told him to gather all the Jews in Susa and tell each one to fast for three days (no food or drinks for anyone), and all of Esther's attendants would do the same. Esther said that she would go to the king after three days. Even though it was against the law, she would risk her life.

You can read through Esther 4 in your Bible for part 4

DAY FOUR

Today's Date: ____________

Who were the three main characters in this chapter?

____

____

____

Questions?

What is sackcloth / why was it worn / why do they dust themselves with ashes?

Sackcloth is a coarsely woven fabric. It was symbolized as a sign of submission or humility before God, and was worn when the Israelites were mourning. The dust and ashes is a reminder of our death, it's a symbol of sorrow for our sins.

What is a fasting?

Fasting is when a person gives up something they commonly use to show God that all we need is Him. Most commonly people fast by not eating or drinking. It is a symbol that we are putting God first.

Give a quick description of what this chapter is about.

____

____

____

____

If you were Esther, would you risk your life by talking to the King?

____

____

____

If you were a Jew, how would you feel if you found out the news about your people?

____

____

What I'm praying about today...

Need ideas? Try praying that God will help you stand strong in tough times.

____

____

____

____

____

____

____

Do not eat or drink for three days, night or day. I and my attendants will fast as you do. When this is done, I will go to the King, even though it is against the law And if I perish, I perish."

- Esther 4:16B, NIV -

This week we are learning about...

Part 5 - Esther's Banquet

Once the Jews had been fasting for three days, Esther put on her royal robe and stood outside of the King's hall where the King was sitting on his royal throne. When he saw Esther standing in the court, he was pleased to see her and held out his golden scepter, so Esther approached him.

Then the king asked, "What is it, Queen Esther? What is your request? Even up to half the kingdom, it will be given you" (Esther 5:3, NIV). Esther, relieved that she was accepted, invited the King and Haman to a banquet she had prepared for them. The King commanded that Haman be brought to him so that they could do what Esther asked.

The King along with Haman attended the banquet that Esther had prepared for them. As they were drinking their wine, the King once again asked Esther what she had wanted. "Even up to half the kingdom, it will be granted," he said to her. Esther replied and told the King that if he regarded her with favor, and if he wanted to grant her request, that the King and Haman would come again the next day to a banquet she would prepare for them. At that time, she would make her request.

Haman in high spirits was walking outside when he noticed Mordecai near the King's gate. When he noticed how Mordecai still refused to show him respect, it filled Haman with rage, but he restrained himself and headed towards home.

Haman liked to show off, and so he gathered his friends and his wife, Zeresh to brag about his wealth, his sons, and all the ways the King admired and honored him. He also told his friends that the Queen had invited him (and only him) to a banquet she held with the King, and that she also invited him to a second banquet the next day. But Haman's high spirits were brought down by Mordecai who sat at the King's gate.

His wife and friends came up with a plan. They told Haman to ask the King in the morning to kill Mordecai where everyone in the city could see. Haman, who was delighted with the idea, set up a tall pole that reached fifty cubits high, in hopes of impaling Mordecai on it. Once Mordecai was killed, Haman would be able to enjoy the banquet with Esther and the King.

You can read through Esther 5 in your Bible for part 5

DAY FIVE

Today's Date: ____________

Congratulations

You've made it half way through an entire book of the Bible!
There are a few extra activities on the next page to recap the past 5 chapters.

How did the King greet Queen Esther who went to visit him without an invitation?

What did the King say he was willing to give to Queen Esther?

What kind of man do you think Haman is? What words would you use to describe him?

God loves it when we pray to Him. You can talk about anything that's on your mind with God.

My prayer of the day...

QUESTIONS / NOTES:

But the Lord is **Faithful** and he will strengthen you and protect you from the evil one.

2 THESSALONIANS 3:3, NIV

Down

2. The King set a royal _ _ _ _ _ on Esther's head.
3. It was customary for a young woman to complete this many months of beauty treatments.
4. How Mordecai and Esther were related.
7. One of the men who plotted to kill the King.
9. Mordecai walked back and forth near the courtyard of the _ _ _ _ _ to find out how Esther was doing.
10. Jew from the tribe of Benjamin.
11. Esther's other name.
13. Original queen in the story.
14. Many of the Jews wore this after finding out about the new decree.
16. A special guard trained to protect the women's living quarters.
19. Appointed as new chief minister.
22. You would be put to _ _ _ _ _ if you saw the King without an invitation.

Across

1. What the King raised to greet Esther into the King's hall.
5. Haman's wife.
6. Esther was made the new _ _ _ _ _ .
8. The king's eunuch who was in charge of the women at the harem.
12. The King served everyone wine in _ _ _ _ cups.
15. The other man caught plotting to kill the King.
17. King in the story.
18. During this time King Ahasuerus was ruler over the ancient city of _ _ _ _ .
20. Haman decided that he was going to _ _ _ _ all of the Jews in the kingdom.
21. One of the king's eunuchs that gave messages to Mordecai from Esther.
23. Esther told all the Jews to _ _ _ _ for three days.
24. Mordecai despised Haman because he was the descendant of an _ _ _ _ _ _ _ _ _ .
25. Esther threw a _ _ _ _ _ _ _ for the King and Haman.

Activity of the day
1
2
3
4
5
6
7
8
9
10
11
12
13
14
15
16
17
18
19
20
21
22
23
24
25
ARE YOU ABLE TO GET THE MESSAGES FROM MORDECAI TO ESTHER?

This week we are learning about...

Part 6 - The King and Mordecai

The King could not sleep that night, so he ordered one of his men to bring him the Book of the Chronicles of the Kings and read it to him. (It was a book with records of his reign). The book mentioned Mordecai, and how he had exposed the two men who plotted to kill the King. The King asked his servant what Mordecai received for his good deed, and the servant replied that Mordecai had not received anything for saving the King.

At this time, Haman entered the outer court of the palace to speak with the King. He wanted to discuss his plot to kill Mordecai and tell the King about the pole he set up. The King ordered his men to bring Haman in and **"when Haman entered, the king asked him, "What should be done for the man the king delights to honor?"** (Esther 6:6, NIV).

In Haman's mind, he didn't think the King honored anyone more than himself. So, Haman answered, saying that the man he wanted to honor should be given a royal robe to wear (one that the King has worn), and that the King's most noble prince should lead him through the city streets on one of the King's horses. By doing this, everyone in the city would know the King was honoring him.

"Go at once," the king commanded Haman. "Get the robe and the horse and do just as you have suggested for Mordecai the Jew, who sits at the king's gate. Do not neglect anything you have recommended" (Esther 6:10, NIV). Disappointed, Haman gathered the robe and horse just as the King commanded, and led Mordecai through the city proclaiming to everyone that the King had honored him.

Haman rushed home afterwards, embarrassed and filled with sorrow. He went to his wife telling her and his friends everything that had happened. His wife said to him **"since Mordecai, before whom your downfall has started, is of Jewish origin, you cannot stand against him—you will surely come to ruin!"** (Esther 6:13B, NIV). And while Haman was talking with his wife, the King's eunuch arrived at the house to take him to the banquet Esther had prepared for him.

You can read through Esther 6 in your Bible for part 6

DAY SIX

Today's Date: ___________

What did the King ask his servant to read to him?
What part of the book did the servant read?

____

____

How do you think Hamen felt when the King said he wanted to honor Mordecai?

____

____

What are some stories you can think of from the Bible where God showed his perfect timing? Give a brief description of the story.

____

____

____

____

When Haman entered, the King asked him, "What should be done for the man the King **DELIGHTS TO HONOR?**" Now Haman thought to himself, "Who is there that the king would rather honor than me?" **(Esther 6:6, NIV)**

Don't you think it's amazing that King Ahasuerus' servant decided to read about what Mordecai had done, just hours before Haman was going to kill him?! Even though we aren't told why the King wasn't able to sleep, we can see that God was working wonders in the story of Esther.

Did you know that it had already been 5 years since Mordecai saved the King? To not have been thanked would have been very unusual at this time. Kings were known to immediately reward people, so for the King to forget was a big deal. Thanks to God's perfect timing, he was rewarded just in time.

This week we are learning about...

Part 7 - Esther's Petition

Haman arrived at the palace for the banquet he had been invited to with the King and Queen. While they sat drinking wine, the King again asked Esther **"Queen Esther, what is your petition? It will be given you. What is your request? Even up to half the kingdom, it will be granted"** (Esther 7:2B, NIV). This time Esther answered the King and asked that if he found favor in her that he would grant her life and spare her people.

Stunned, the King asked Esther who and where the man was who dared to do such a thing. Esther replied and said "An adversary and enemy! This vile Haman!"

Haman trembled with fear before the King and Queen. The King, filled with rage, stood up and went out into the palace garden while Haman stayed behind begging Queen Esther for his life. The King returned to the banquet hall and found Haman who was falling on the couch where Esther was reclining. As you can imagine, the King was angry!

Haman's face was quickly covered by the servants. Then Harbona, one of the King's eunuchs attending the King suggested a plan, **"A pole reaching to a height of fifty cubits stands by Haman's house. He had it set up for Mordecai, who spoke up to help the king"** (Esther 7:9, NIV) and so the King decided to punish Haman instead on the very same trap that was set up for Mordecai.

You can read through Esther 7 in your Bible for part 7

My Prayer of The Day

____

____

____

____

____

DAY SEVEN

Today's Date: ____________

NOTES / QUESTIONS: ____________

____

____

____

Activity of the day

Today we are going to be taking a break from the questions and jump into some Bible Trivia! Match up the name of the person you think the sentence applies to. Answers are in the chapters of Esther found in this book.

1. ________ One of the King's eunuchs that gave messages to Mordecai.
2. ________ Put on a royal robe and stood outside of the King's hall without an invitation.
3. ________ Didn't think the King honored anyone more than him.
4. ________ Tore off his clothes and replaced them with sackcloth.
5. ________ Asked the King if he would spare the lives of her people.
6. ________ Begged Queen Esther for his life.
7. ________ Haman's wife.
8. ________ Tried sending clothes to Mordecai.
9. ________ Offered up to half the kingdom to Esther.
10. ________ Led through the city on a horse while wearing the King's robe.
11. ________ One of the King's eunuchs that reminded the King about the pole Haman had set up.
12. ________ Attended a banquet with the King that Esther prepared.

Names to match up:

(And yes, they can be reused)

A - Harbona
B - Haman
C - Mordecai
E - Ahasuerus
F - Esther
G - Hathak
D - Zeresh

This week we are learning about...

Part 8 - The New Order

Esther revealed her history to the King and told him of her and Mordecai's relationship. That same day King Ahasuerus handed over the estate that was once Haman's to Esther and took back his signet ring which he then gave to Mordecai. Esther also gave Mordecai the estate that the King had given to her.

Although Haman was no longer in the story, the plan to kill the Jews was still in effect. Esther fell to the King's feet weeping, and begged him to put an end to Haman's plan. The King extended his gold scepter to Esther, and she stood up in front of the King and asked him, "If you respect me and think it's the right thing to do, please reverse the order to destroy my people."

The King replied to Esther and to Mordecai who was with him. He told them to write another decree in the King's name on behalf of the Jews. They were instructed to seal it with the King's signet ring. (No document written in the King's name and sealed with his ring can be revoked.)

The royal secretaries were summoned and wrote out all of Mordecai's new orders regarding the Jews. All the orders were written in the name of the King and sealed with the King's signet ring which he had given to Mordecai. The new order granted Jews the right to assemble and protect themselves and were free from Haman's evil plan against them. The King's new order for the Jews also gave them the right to protect themselves. It gave them the right to destroy anyone that might attack them or their families.

There was a specific day appointed for the Jews to have their revenge (thirteenth day of the twelfth month). A copy of the new order was issued as law in every province and all of the Jews prepared themselves.

Mordecai left the King's presence wearing royal garments, a gold crown, and a purple robe of fine linen. The city held a celebration and for the Jews it was a joyous and happy time.

You can read through Esther 8 in your Bible for part 8

DAY EIGHT

Today's Date: ______________

What were the five things that the King and Queen gave Mordecai?

____

____

What does it mean when the King holds out his gold scepter?

____

____

MY PRAYER OF THE DAY: ______________________

____

____

____

This week we are learning about...

When the thirteenth day of the twelfth month arrived, the enemies of the Jews who originally thought they had the upper hand were wrong. The Jews overpowered them and the tables had now turned against the people who had wished harm against them.

Jews from all provinces of the King assembled, determined to destroy those who were teamed up to attack them. But, no one could stand against the Jews because everyone in all of the provinces were afraid of them. The nobles, satraps, governors and the King's administrators all helped the Jews because of fear of Mordecai's new power. Mordecai had made a name for himself in the palace and his reputation had spread throughout the city as he became more and more powerful.

The Jews destroyed all of their enemies, and in the citadel of Susa, the Jews had killed and destroyed five hundred men. Later that day, when the King heard how many people had lost their lives in the city, he went to the Queen and told her. The King then said to her **"Now what is your petition? It will be given you. What is your request? It will also be granted"** (Esther 9:12B, NIV). Esther asked that the King give the Jews in Susa permission to carry out the order for one more day and to let Haman's ten sons be punished just as Haman had been. The King agreed and an edict was issued in Susa.

The Jews struck down the ten sons of Haman. Their names were Parshandatha, Dalphon, Aspatha, Poratha, Adalia, Aridatha, Parmashta, Arisai, Aridai and Vaizatha. But the Jews made sure not to lay a hand on any of their possessions or money.

On the fourteenth day of that month, the Jews destroyed a total of three hundred more men in Susa, but again they did not lay a hand on any of their possessions or money. Outside of the city, in the King's other provinces, Jews had destroyed seventy-five thousand of their enemies on the first day. On the second day, the fourteenth, they all rested and celebrated with feasting and joy. (after this, Jews started to observe the thirteenth and fourteenth of the month as a day of joy and feasting, a day for giving presents to each other.)

This beautiful story concludes by reminding us of the goodness of God and His miraculous work in the life of Mordecai. He will forever be remembered in The Chronicles of the Kings, and of course in each one of our hearts.

Because of his faithfulness and goodness to God's people, Mordecai was exalted above men, second only to the King. What a reminder he is of our Lord and Savior Jesus who loved us so much that He died on the cross. The Bible tells us that Jesus, like Mordecai is exalted above all men. And like Mordecai who reigned with the King. Jesus sits at the right hand of God, where He reigns with His father in heaven.

You can read through Esther 9–10 in your Bible for part 9

DAY NINE

Today's Date: ____________

INTERESTING FACT: The book of Esther has a total of 10 chapters. The tenth chapter in the book is only 3 verses long! Even though it is extremely short, it still isn't the shortest chapter in the Bible.

Psalm 117 has only two verses in it and is the shortest chapter in the entire Bible. Esther Chapter 10 makes for the second smallest chapter in the Bible.

There were a total of 127 provinces in the KING'S KINGDOM

What did Esther ask the King?

____

____

How many men did the Jews destroy in Susa on the thirteenth?
How many men did the Jews destroy in Susa on the fourteenth?

____

____

What do the Jews do on the fourteenth and fifteenth day of the twelfth month every year? (Read through Esther 9:20-22)

____

____

How has the character of Mordecai changed since the first chapter?

____

____

____

____

My Prayer of The Day

____

____

____

____

How great are his signs,
how mighty his wonders!
His kingdom is an
eternal kingdom;
his dominion endures from
generation to generation
– Daniel 4:3, NIV –

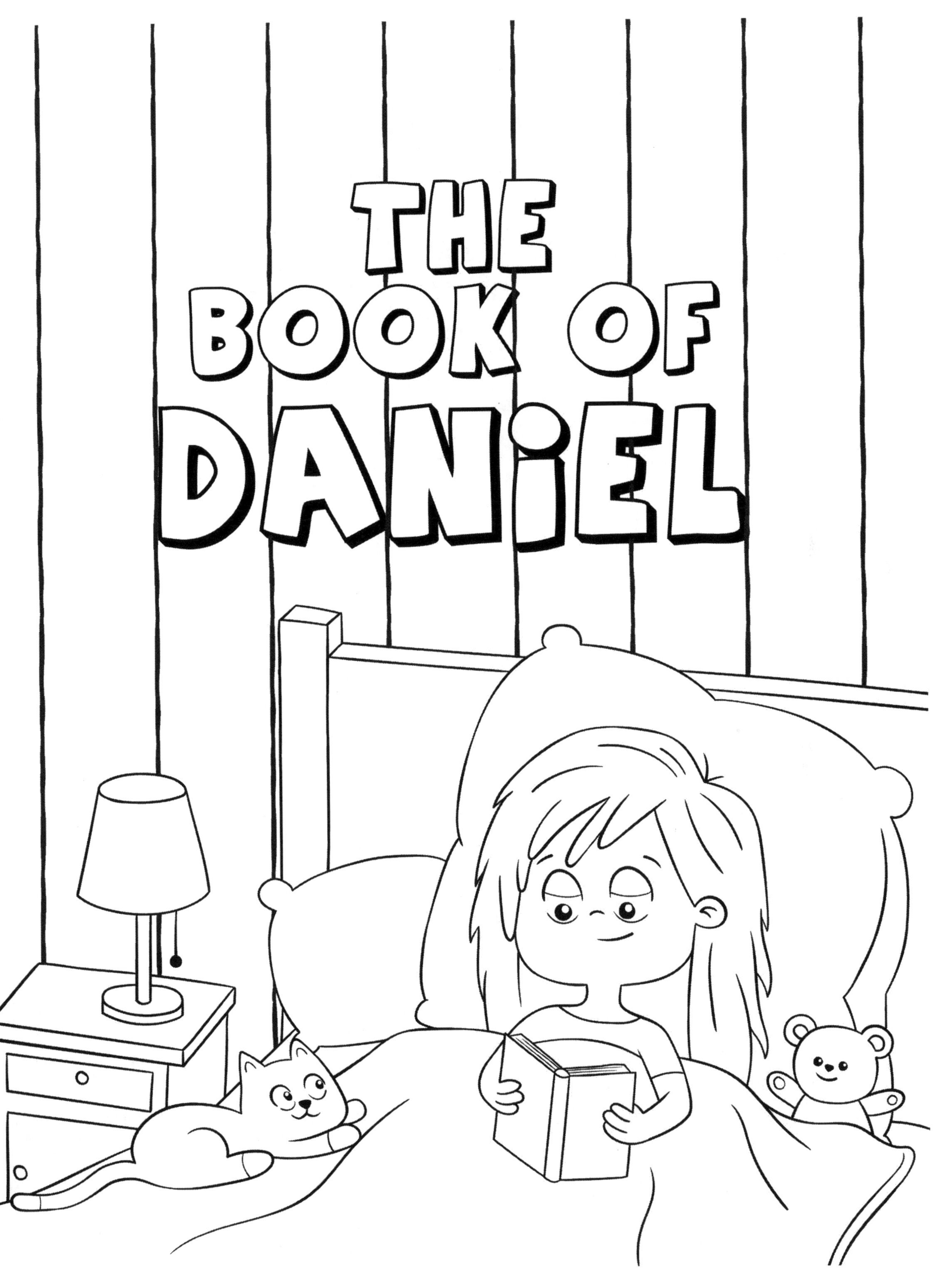
THE
BOOK OF
DANiEL

This week we are learning about...

Daniel in the Lion's Den

King Darius ruled over the land of Babylon and had picked a hundred and twenty of the very best people in the kingdom to help him rule. He then picked three of them to be in charge, one of whom was Daniel.

Daniel was the leader of advisors and was a man who believed in God and followed his commands. The other men that were in charge did not like Daniel and did not want him in charge, so they came up with a plan to get rid of him.

The men went to King Darius and suggested a new law in which people could worship and pray to only the King and if they worshipped or prayed to other gods, they would be thrown into the lion's den.

Daniel heard about the new law but decided he would still pray to God and praise the Lord. He prayed multiple times a day, and when the other men saw him praying through an open window, they told King Darius. The king was very upset by the news. He favored Daniel and did not want to harm him, but because he had broken the law he was to be punished. Before sending Daniel to the hungry lions, King Darius said to him, "May the God that you worship, rescue you!"

When the King returned to his palace that night he was unable to eat or sleep. In the morning, the King hurried to the lion's den and called out for Daniel. "Daniel, did God save you? Did the Lord rescue you?" he asked.

Daniel answered by telling the King that God sent an angel to shut the mouths of of the lions. He wasn't even scratched, because God knew that Daniel was a faithful servant. King Darius was filled with joy and ordered his men to take Daniel out of the den. Because of God's faithfulness, Daniel wasn't hurt at all.

The King then commanded that the men who had falsely accused Daniel were to be thrown in with the lions. He issued a decree that everyone in the kingdom had to fear and honor Daniel's God.

"For he is the living God and he endures forever; his kingdom will not be destroyed, his dominion will never end. He rescues and he saves; he performs signs and wonders in the heavens and on the earth. He has rescued Daniel from the power of the lions."

(Daniel 6:26-27, NIV)

Read through **Daniel 6** for the story

DAY ONE

Today's Date: ____________

What has this story taught you? ____

The story of Daniel in the lion's den teaches us that even if we feel like everything has been lost, God will always be there for us keeping us safe from harm.

QUESTIONS I HAVE

You can ask a parent, friend, or someone from church to help you

Activity of the day

A	E	O	W	D	E	U	C	S	E	R	I	U	S	X
N	K	G	O	D	P	O	A	I	M	V	D	L	R	B
J	I	Q	U	E	C	O	W	Z	Y	S	A	H	O	I
Y	N	A	V	H	W	O	R	S	H	I	P	O	K	R
F	D	B	L	L	J	S	T	D	A	R	I	R	T	A
Y	A	K	I	G	F	L	A	T	W	D	A	G	U	D
A	W	O	R	P	K	R	E	G	D	A	L	W	S	Q
R	N	Z	V	E	I	A	L	R	N	R	P	Z	D	P
P	M	E	O	C	N	E	A	T	F	I	A	C	E	O
O	K	A	C	C	I	V	O	L	B	U	K	R	C	A
C	R	M	P	N	F	R	E	I	U	S	H	I	W	A
P	R	A	A	Z	E	T	G	A	L	I	O	A	A	C
X	E	D	R	I	N	O	L	Y	B	A	B	I	L	U
R	E	S	C	U	G	D	U	A	R	P	W	B	A	A

DANIEL
DARIUS
GOD
KING
PRAY
LION
BABYLON
WORSHIP
LAW
RESCUED

DAY TWO

Today's Date: ____________

Yesterday we talked about how God will always be there for us. What are some ways that you know God is there for you?

____
____
____
____

"Now when Daniel learned that the decree had been published, he went home to his upstairs room where the windows opened toward Jerusalem. Three times a day he got down on his knees and prayed, giving thanks to his God, just as he had done before."

– **Daniel 6:10, NIV** –

Praying to God is very important. It's our time to talk about what's on our mind. What are some things you talk to God about?

____
____
____
____
____
____
____
____

Things I am

thankful for ...

1. ____________________
2. ____________________
3. ____________________
4. ____________________

It is important for us to give thanks to God. One of the ways we do that is through prayer.

Activity of the day

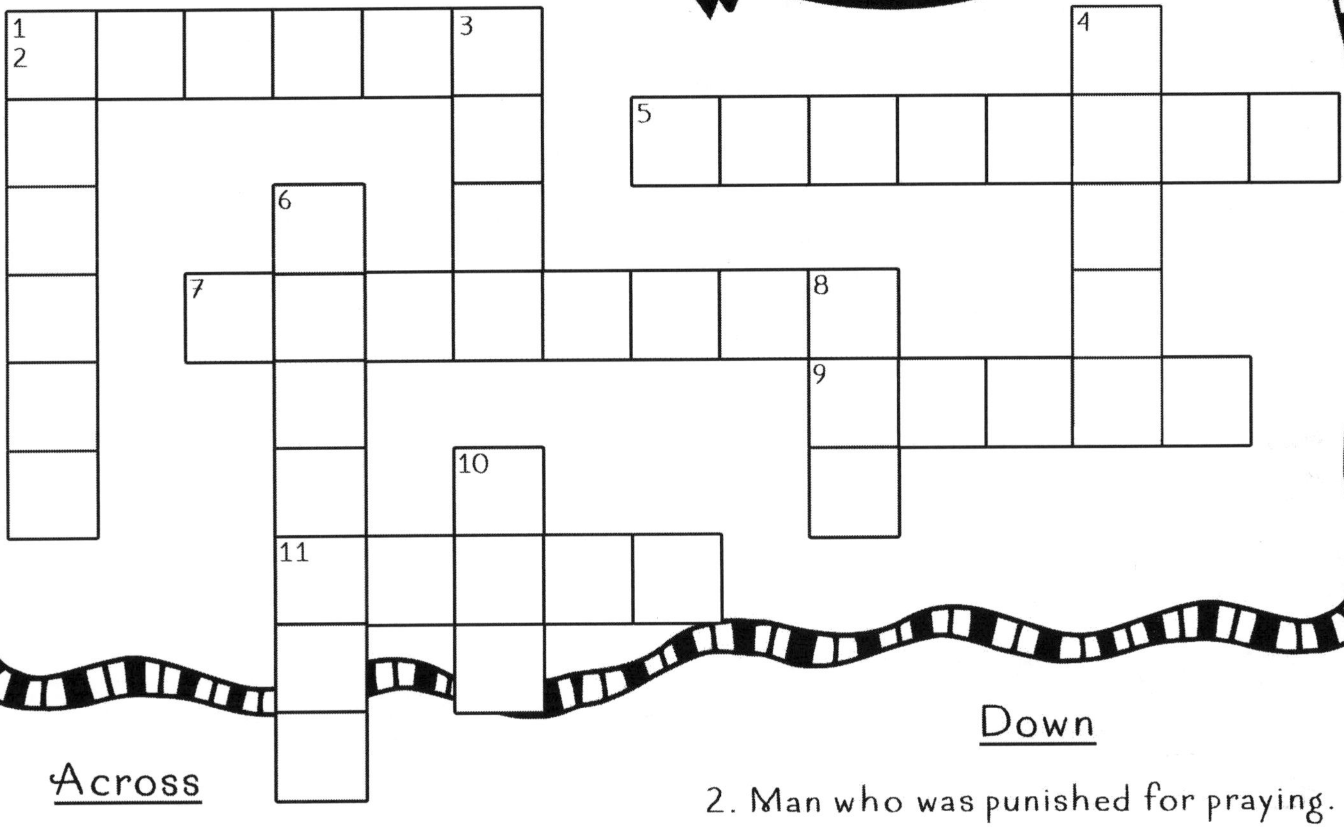

Across

1. The king who was ruling.
5. Because Daniel broke the law, he was to be _ _ _ _ _ _ _ _.
7. God protected Daniel because he was _ _ _ _ _ _ _ _ to him.
9. What did God send Daniel in the den?
11. Daniel was thrown into a den of _ _ _ _ _.

Down

2. Man who was punished for praying.
3. God _ _ _ _ the mouths of the lions.
4. How many times did Daniel pray everyday?
6. The king ruled over _ _ _ _ _ _ _.
8. King Darius changed this so that people could only pray to him.
10. King Darius was filled with _ _ _ when he went to see Daniel the next morning.

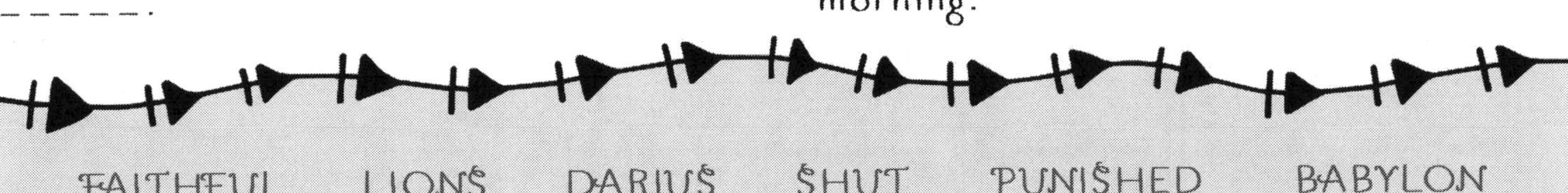

DAY THREE Today's Date: ____________

The Bible can teach us so many lessons.
Has the story of Daniel taught you anything new about God?

____
____
____
____

For I am the Lord your God who takes hold of your right hand and says to you, Do not fear; I will help you.

– Isaiah 41:13, NIV –

Daniel showed everyone his faith through prayer. He was a man of God, and everyone around him knew it.

What are some ways you show your Christianity to people around you?

____
____
____
____
____
____

(Do you do kind deeds for strangers, help out at church, or talk to your friends about God?)

What I'm praying about today...

Need ideas? Try, I praise You for... I'm sorry for... Please help me...

____
____
____
____
____
____
____
____

"He answered their prayers, because they **trusted** in him.

– 1 Chronicles 5:20, NIV –"

The king was OVERJOYED and gave orders to lift Daniel out of the den. And when Daniel was lifted from the den, no wound was found on him, because he had TRUSTED IN HIS GOD.
Daniel 6:23, NIV

But I, with shouts of
grateful praise, will sacrifice
to you. What I have vowed
I will make good. I will say,
'Salvation
comes from
the Lord.'
– Jonah 2:9, NIV –

THE
BOOK OF
JONAH

This week we are learning about...

The Story of Jonah

Jonah, a prophet during this time, was sent a message from the Lord. God told him to travel to the city of Nineveh and preach to them because they had become sinful and wicked.

However, Jonah ran away from God and headed for the sea where he found a ship. He got on and set sail for Tarshish. After the boat had left, God sent a wind over the sea and a violent storm arose that threatened to break the ship. The people were afraid and each prayed to his own god. But Jonah had gone below the deck where he went to sleep. One of the men found him and pleaded for him to pray to God. Then one of the sailors suggested that they cast lots to find the person responsible for the storm. The lot fell on Jonah and the men cornered him asking many questions.

Jonah explained that he was a Hebrew and that he worshiped the Lord. This made the men very scared because they knew he was running from God. So they asked Jonah what they had to do to calm the sea. He answered and told them to throw him into the sea, and the storm would calm. But the men didn't listen. They tried to row back to land instead. God made the storm heavier and it was impossible for the men to escape so they prayed to God and asked that they would not be punished if they threw Jonah into the water. Then all the men took Jonah and threw him overboard into the sea and it was calm once again. The men feared the Lord because they knew that He was in control.

When Jonah fell into the sea, God sent a huge fish to swallow him up. Jonah was in the belly of the fish for three days and three nights, where he prayed to the Lord and praised him. The Lord heard, and released Jonah from the fish's belly.

Once again the Lord sent a message to Jonah. He told him to go to Nineveh and give them the proclamation that he was to give before.

"This is the proclamation he issued in Nineveh: "By the decree of the king and his nobles: Do not let people or animals, herds or flocks, taste anything; do not let them eat or drink. But let people and animals be covered with sackcloth. Let everyone call urgently on God. Let them give up their evil ways and their violence. Who knows? God may yet relent and with compassion turn from his fierce anger so that we will not perish." (Jonah 3:7-9, NIV)

This time Jonah obeyed God's word and he went. It took Jonah three days to travel through the city. He walked through the city proclaiming that it was to be overthrown. The people believed Jonah. When his warning reached the King of Nineveh, he took off his royal clothing and covered himself in sackcloth, as did everyone in the city, and he sat down in the dust.

God saw that they listened and turned from their evil ways, so He changed His mind and did not destroy them as He said that He would.

Read through Jonah 1-3 to see the full story in your Bible.

DAY ONE

Today's Date: ______________

JONAH RUNS FROM GOD

What did God ask Jonah to do?

___

___

___

Do you know what a prophet is? It is a person who delivers messages from God. A well known prophet we've talked about is Moses who delivered the Ten Commandments from God.

Why do you think Jonah choose not to listen to God?

___

___

What did Jonah decide to do instead of listening to God?

___

___

___

KEY PLACES

Gath-Hepher: a small border town where Jonah is from.

Joppa: a seaport where Jonah boarded a ship.

DID YOU KNOW? Jonah was the only biblical prophet to run from his call.

Questions I have:

___

___

___

___

___

My Prayer of The Day

Need ideas? Try, "thank you Lord for," "please help me with," "I'm sorry for..."

___

___

___

___

___

DAY TWO

Today's Date: ____________

JONAH BOARDS A SHIP

KEY PLACES

Tarshish: Jonah's intended destination.

Joppa: a seaport where Jonah boarded a ship.

What did God send after Jonah once he had gotten on the boat?

Where and what was Jonah doing while everyone was praying?

What is casting lots?

Casting lots was a method people used to determine the "will of God". They were either sticks or stones with markings and they were thrown into a small area where the results were interpreted. Kind of like if you were to use dice!

Why were the men scared when Jonah told them who he was?

Instead of throwing Jonah into the sea, what did the men try to do? Did it work?

What did the men end up doing to calm the sea?

What did Jonah do inside the fish, and how did he get out?

Questions I have:

My Prayer of The Day

DAY THREE

Today's Date: ____________

JONAH DELIVERS A MESSAGE

KEY PLACES

Nineveh: Capital city of the Assyrian Empire, located on the Tigris River where Jonah went to send a message from God.

What did God ask Jonah to do after He had saved him from the belly of the fish?

How many times did God ask Jonah to go to Nineveh?

How did the people respond to the proclamation? What did the people and the King do?

Once God had seen how the people acted what did He do?

What do you think the story of Jonah teaches us about God's will?

Questions I have:

DID YOU KNOW? One of the four Old Testament prophets that Jesus referred to in the New Testament was Jonah. The others were Elijah, Elisha, and Isaiah.

(In the book of Matthew 12:41)

MY PRAYER OF THE DAY:

Activity of the day

All of the answers can be found in this book.

DOWN

1. The men on the boat were busy _______ to their gods.
3. Jonah's intended destination.
6. Jonah was __________ by a large fish.
8. What the people put on when Jonah came to Nineveh.
9. Jonah was one of the four ___ __________ prophets that Jesus referred to.
10. God issued a _____________ to Nineveh.
12. The seaport where Jonah boarded a ship.
14. Amount of days and nights Jonah was in the belly of the fish.

ACROSS

2. What Jonah boarded.
4. Below deck Jonah was ________.
5. What swallowed Jonah.
7. The men threw Jonah into the ___.
11. Casting ____ was a method people used to determine the "will of God."
13. The book of the Bible this story took place in.
15. The small border town where Jonah is from.
16. Capital city of the Assyrian Empire, located on the Tigris River where Jonah went to send a message from God.

Do to
others as you would
have them

do to you

Luke 6:31, NIV

THE BOOK OF LUKE

This week we are learning about...

The Birth of Jesus - Part 1

An Angel Appears to Mary

Long ago, in the northern town of Nazareth, there lived a young woman named Mary who was engaged to a man named Joseph. One day God sent the Angel Gabriel to send a message to Mary. He told her that God had blessed her and she was soon to be pregnant. She would give birth to a baby boy named Jesus. He would be God's son. Mary was afraid, but she trusted God. Gabriel told Mary that her cousin Elizabeth, who everyone thought was too old to have children, would also be having a baby boy. The baby would prepare the people to welcome Jesus, and he was going to be named John.

After hearing the news, Mary went to see her cousin Elizabeth and her husband Zechariah. She told them what the angel had told her, but they already heard the good news. An angel had appeared to Zechariah and told him about the baby that they were to have. Mary ended up staying with Elizabeth for three months, and then she returned home to Nazareth.

When Joseph found out that Mary was expecting a child he was worried. They were not married yet, and he wondered if they should put off the wedding. An angel then appeared to Joseph in his dream and told him not to be afraid. The angel told Joseph that Mary had been chosen by God and that the baby would be the Saviour of the world.

DAY ONE

Today's Date: ____________

Where did Mary and Joseph live? ____________________________

Which angel did God send to see Mary? ____________________________

What did the angel say about Elizabeth?

____

____

How long did Mary stay with Elizabeth and her husband? ____________

What was Joseph's reaction to finding out Mary would be pregnant?

____

____

Questions I have: ____________________________

____

____

N A G A B R I E L I U S J
J M S E J D J R P J P E E
O E A O G O E D F E R N L
H R A R H R N N M S E G I
O P B N Y S A A J U G A Z
A L G J O B Z N E S N H A
N E D E N G A G E D A F B
S G L E A R R B E M N U E
A N G N A E E N Y B T L T
O A U E B R T E A N B N H
E J O S E P H B S O J A M
O R J A E R U O I V A S G

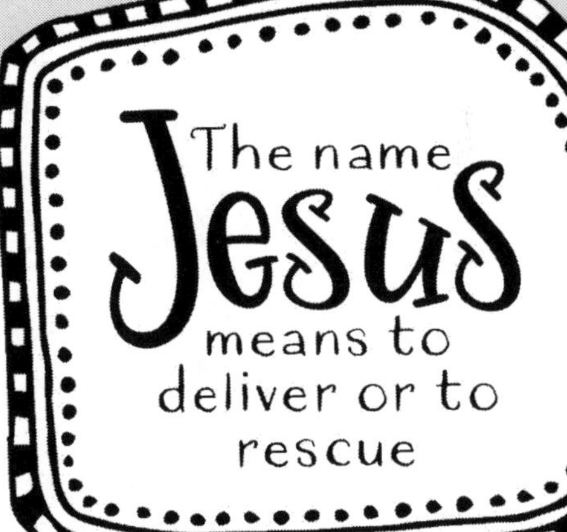

NAZARETH
MARY
ENGAGED
JOSEPH
ANGEL
GABRIEL
PREGNANT
JESUS
JOHN
ELIZABETH
BABY
SAVIOUR

This week we are learning about...

The Birth of Jesus - Part 2

Jesus is Born

Joseph believed the angel and when he woke up he married Mary. During this time the Roman Emperor Augustus called for everyone to return to their home towns and enter their names in a registry so that the government could have a list of all the people in the empire. Mary and Joseph traveled to Bethlehem where they ended up staying in a barn since there were no rooms available at the time. While they were there, Mary gave birth, and she wrapped her baby in cloth and placed him in one of the mangers.

That night there were shepherds out in their fields nearby watching over their flocks when an angel appeared. The shepherds were terrified, but the angel told them to not be afraid. "Do not be afraid," he said. "I'm bringing good news with great joy for all of the people." The angel also told them about the Saviour that had been born in Bethlehem. Then the sky lit up with many more angels as they praised God.

When the angel left, the shepherds decided to go to Bethlehem and visit the baby who the Lord had told them about. They quickly went on their way and found Mary and Joseph with the baby wrapped in cloth and sleeping in the manger. The men spread the news of the Saviour being born, and everyone that heard the story was amazed.

DAY TWO

Today's Date: ____________

Were the shepherds afraid when they saw the angel?

____

What did the angel tell them?

____

____

What did the shepherds do after the angel left?

____

____

Down

1. God told Mary that she was going to be _ _ _ _ _ _ _ _ with a child.
3. Jesus was wrapped in cloth and placed in a _ _ _ _ _ _.
4. Mary's husband.
6. Appeared to the shepherds in their field.

Across

2. Woman God chose to be Jesus' mom.
5. The angel told Joseph that the baby was going to be a _ _ _ _ _ _ _.
7. Name, meaning to deliver or to rescue.
8. Where Mary and Joseph traveled to
9. Spread the news of the Saviour being born.

For to us a child is born, to us a son is given, and the government will be on his shoulders. And he will be called Wonderful Counselor, Mighty God, Everlasting Father,

PRINCE OF PEACE

– Isaiah 9:6, NIV –

1 2 3 4 5 6 7 8 9

This week we are learning about...

The Birth of Jesus - Part 3

The Three Wise Men

At the time when Jesus was born, a brand-new star had appeared in the sky. Wise men who had studied stars had known stories of a new star appearing when a great king was born. They gathered gifts for Jesus and followed the star towards the country of Judea. When they got to the capital, Jerusalem, they asked if anyone knew where the baby was. The king of Judea, Herod, heard the news of the wise men and it made him very angry to think of someone taking his place.

Herod met with the wise men and told them to keep following the star until they had found the baby. Once they found him, they were to return and let him know where he was, so that he would be able to go and worship the new king. But, Herod was an evil man who had other plans which he told no one of.

The wise men followed the star to Bethlehem, where it shined directly down on the place where Jesus was. When they arrived, the wise men bowed and worshiped Jesus. They spread out the gifts they had brought to Him. The gifts were gold, frankincense and myrrh. God had appeared to the wise men in a dream and told them not to go back to Herod, and so they listened and each returned back to their country.

Once the wise men left, an angel appeared to Joseph in a dream. The angel warned him to get up, take his wife and Jesus, and escape to Egypt, because king Herod was looking for them. Herod was angry once he realized the wise men were not returning. Joseph got up quickly, and left for Egypt with Mary and Jesus during the night. They stayed there until Herod died.

Once Herod died. another angel appeared to Joseph in a dream and told him to take Mary and Jesus back to Israel because they no longer feared anyone coming after Jesus. When Joseph and his family went back to Israel, they found out that Herod's son was now king. They were afraid to stay so they returned to Galilee and lived in their old town of Nazareth.

DAY THREE

Today's Date: ____________

NOTES / QUESTIONS: ____________________

____

____

____

Activity of the day

Today we are going to be taking a break from the questions and jumping into some Bible Trivia! Match up the name of the person you think each sentence applies to. Answers can be found in parts 1, 2, and 3 of this book.

1. ________ Followed a star to Bethlehem.
2. ________ Roman Emperor.
3. ________ An angel appeared to them while they were in their field.
4. ________ Placed in a manger.
5. ________ Even in her old age, God was going to bless her with a baby.
6. ________ King of Judea.
7. ____&____ Traveled to Bethlehem and couldn't find a room to rent.
8. ________ Brought gifts for the new baby.
9. ________ Angel sent to speak with Mary.
10. ________ When he found out that Mary was expecting a child he was worried.
11. ________ Warned Joseph to take his family and escape to Egypt.
12. ________ An angel appeared and told him about the baby his wife Elizabeth was going to have.
13. ________ Told Joseph to take his family to Israel.
14. ________ When he was born, a brand new star appeared in the sky.
15. ________ Went to Bethlehem to visit the baby first.
16. ________ The baby born to prepare the people to welcome Jesus.

Names to match up:

(And yes, they can be reused)

A - Jesus
B - Herod
C - Wise Men
D - Angel
E - Augustus
F - Mary
G - Joseph
H - Shepherds
I - Gabriel
J - Elizabeth
K - John
L - Zechariah

This week we are learning about...

Zacchaeus the Tax Collector

One day when Jesus was passing through Jericho, a man by the name of Zacchaeus was there. Zacchaeus was a chief tax collector and was very wealthy. During these times tax collectors were rich, powerful, and known to take advantage of people. Zacchaeus wanted to see Jesus as He passed through Jericho. Since he was too short to see over the crowd, Zacchaeus climbed a sycamore tree that was up ahead so that he would be able to get a clear view of Jesus.

When Jesus arrived at the spot where Zacchaeus was, He looked up to him, called him down, and even asked Zacchaeus if he could go to his house. As Zacchaeus hurried down and welcomed Jesus, all the people that were around began complaining saying, "He's going to a sinner's house!"

But Zacchaeus changed in that moment. He stood up and told the Lord that he was going to give half of his possessions to the poor, and he was going to pay back four times the amount of anything he had cheated anyone out of.

"Jesus said to him, "Today salvation has come to this house, because this man, too, is a son of Abraham. For the Son of Man came to seek and to save the lost." (Luke 19:9-10, NIV)

You can read through **Luke 19:1-10** in your Bible

Activity of the day

ZACCHAEUS
SHORT
JESUS
SINNER
JERICHO
WEALTHY
TREE
CLIMBED

```
Z J R E I S R A E S T G E S E
E A E S W E N N I U S R L J S
S M C R I E F I T S D L E R A
H J A C I N A R E E H I O E L
O E I L N C I L B J L E L N K
R R W E A E H M T C T A W N C
T T G V J S I O I H L N G I O
H C L E B L E R T A Y A O S T
S Z A C C H A E U S N H E L E
I E P T R L C C T I S N E W E
```

How would you describe the character of Zacchaeus?

What did Zacchaeus do when he saw Jesus?

Why didn't people like Zacchaeus?

What can we learn from how Jesus treated Zacchaeus?
What does this story teach us about being Christians?

What did Zacchaeus say he was going to do?

My Prayer of the Day

For God so loved the world that he gave
his one and only Son, that whoever
believes in him shall not
perish but have
eternal
life
John 3:16, NIV

THE
BOOK OF
JOHN

This week we are learning about...

Jesus Turns Water Into Wine

Jesus was able to do the unimaginable as we can see in all of His stories. He healed the sick and performed acts that no other human could possibly do. In the Book of Luke, we see a short story about Jesus turning water into wine.

Jesus and his mother Mary had gone to a wedding in Galilee. Also attending the wedding were Jesus' disciples. When the wine had been used all up Mary went to Jesus and told him. Nearby were six water jars, each holding twenty to thirty gallons. Jesus told the servants at the wedding to fill jars up to the brim with water, and then told them to draw some of the water out and to take it to the master of the banquet.

The servants did what Jesus said and took the water to the master of the banquet. He had not realized it was once water and the servant was the only one who knew where it had come from. He then called the groom and asked him why he had saved the best wine for last.

You can read through **Luke 2:1-11** for the story of Jesus turning water into wine.

DAY ONE

Today's Date: ____________

What kind of event were Jesus and his mother attending?

___

What did Mary tell Jesus?

___

What did Jesus do about it?

___

If each jar could hold up to 30 gallons, how many gallons of wine were made?

___

What was the groom's reaction after tasting the wine?

___

The Bible says that by Jesus turning water into wine, He revealed His glory and His disciples then believed in Him. Jesus is able to do miraculous things that we couldn't even imagine. No problem we have is too big for Him to fix.

Activity of the day

Jesus looked at them and said, "With man this is impossible, but with God all things are possible. **Matthew 19:26, NIV**

This week we are learning about...

The Parable of the Lost Sheep

Do you know what a parable is?
It's a story that Jesus uses to teach a lesson. Even though they are very simple stories there are strong meanings behind them. In this chapter, we are going to be talking about The Parable of the Lost Sheep. It is a story Jesus told in the Book of Luke.

Jesus was talking and visiting with tax collectors and sinners. The tax collectors, who thought they were righteous in Jesus' eyes, started to whisper to each other about Jesus and how they didn't think He should be eating with the sinners. Jesus knew what the men were thinking and decided to tell them a story.

"Suppose one of you has a hundred sheep and loses one of them. Doesn't he leave the ninety-nine in the open country and go after the lost sheep until he finds it? And when he finds it, he joyfully puts it on his shoulders and goes home. Then he calls his friends and neighbors together and says, 'Rejoice with me; I have found my lost sheep.' I tell you that in the same way there will be more rejoicing in heaven over one sinner who repents than over ninety-nine righteous persons who do not need to repent."

- Luke 15:4-7, NIV -

QUESTIONS I HAVE: ________________________

____

____

____

NOTES: ________________________

____

____

____

____

____

____

____

You can read through **Luke 15:1-7**

What is it that Jesus is trying to tell the tax collectors and sinners?
What does this story mean to you?

____

____

____

____

Who does a shepherd do when loses one of his sheep?

____

____

What does this story teach you about God's love for you?

____

____

G U Y A O I A S G L U I I S
R J G H S E A P E E H S Z I
Q E M U N P C O W D F G B N
Y A P L U K E R E P E E J N
L J O E D N E S S E C I R E F
O E K V N E L A L N D A F R L
V S S T D T S B N D S G T S O
F U I O L U A R R O E T K U L
R S U Z P R A A P N S Y C L T
U J L G A E C U T E R S R R N
I E Y P B E R L I O S H E E O
T R O R T R E G T L P T A L C
B G S H E N O S I B A B H S F

For this is what the Sovereign Lord says: I myself will search for my sheep and look after them.

– Ezekiel 34:11, NIV –

SHEEP	PARABLE
JESUS	LESSON
LUKE	SINNERS
STORY	REPENT

DAY TWO

Today's Date: ____________

<<<—>>>—<<<—>>>—<<<—>>> <<<—>>>

Yesterday we talked about The Parable of the Lost Sheep but did you know there is also the Parable of the Wandering Sheep in the book of Matthew? Having the two stories helps us to see things from a different angle.

"See that you do not despise one of these little ones. For I tell you that their angels in heaven always see the face of my Father in heaven. "What do you think? If a man owns a hundred sheep, and one of them wanders away, will he not leave the ninety-nine on the hills and go to look for the one that wandered off? And if he finds it, truly I tell you, he is happier about that one sheep than about the ninety-nine that did not wander off. In the same way your Father in heaven is not willing that any of these little ones should perish.

- Matthew 18:10-14, NIV -

The parable from Luke is very similar to the parable from Matthew. What similarities do you notice in the two stories?

____

____

____

In the two stories, what do the sheep represent?

____

____

Have you ever experienced a time when you felt like you wandered from God?

____

____

And if he finds it, truly I tell you, he is happier about that one sheep than about the ninety-nine that did not wander off. In the same way your Father in heaven is not willing that any of these little ones should perish.

- Matthew 18:13, NIV -

What I'm praying about today...

Need ideas? Try praying for someone you know who might need God's love in their life.

____

____

____

____

____

____

Down

1. We all, like sheep, have gone ______, each of us has turned to our own way; and the Lord has laid on him the iniquity of us all. **(Isaiah 53:6, NIV)**

2. My sheep listen to my _____; I know them, and they follow me. **(John 10:27, NIV)**

3. For this is what the _________ Lord says: I myself will search for my sheep and look after them. **(Ezekiel 34:11, NIV)**

4. I will search for the lost and bring back the strays. I will bind up the injured and strengthen the weak, but the sleek and the strong I will destroy. I will shepherd the flock with _______. **(Ezekiel 34:16, NIV)**

9. I form the light and create darkness, I bring prosperity and create disaster; I, the ____, do all these things. **(Isaiah 45:7, NIV)**

Across

5. I tell you that in the same way there will be more _________ in heaven over one sinner who repents than over ninety-nine righteous persons who do not need to repent. **(Luke 15:7, NIV)**

6. I am the good shepherd. The good shepherd lays down his life for the _____. **(John 10:11, NIV)**

7. ______, for the kingdom of heaven has come near. **(Matthew 3:2, NIV)**

8. For God so loved the world that he gave his one and only Son, that whoever believes in him shall not perish but have _______ life. **(John 3:16, NIV)**

10. What, then, shall we say in response to these things? If ___ is for us, who can be against us? **(Romans 8:31, NIV)**

Since we live
by the Spirit,
let us keep in
step with the
Spirit

Galatians 5:25, NIV

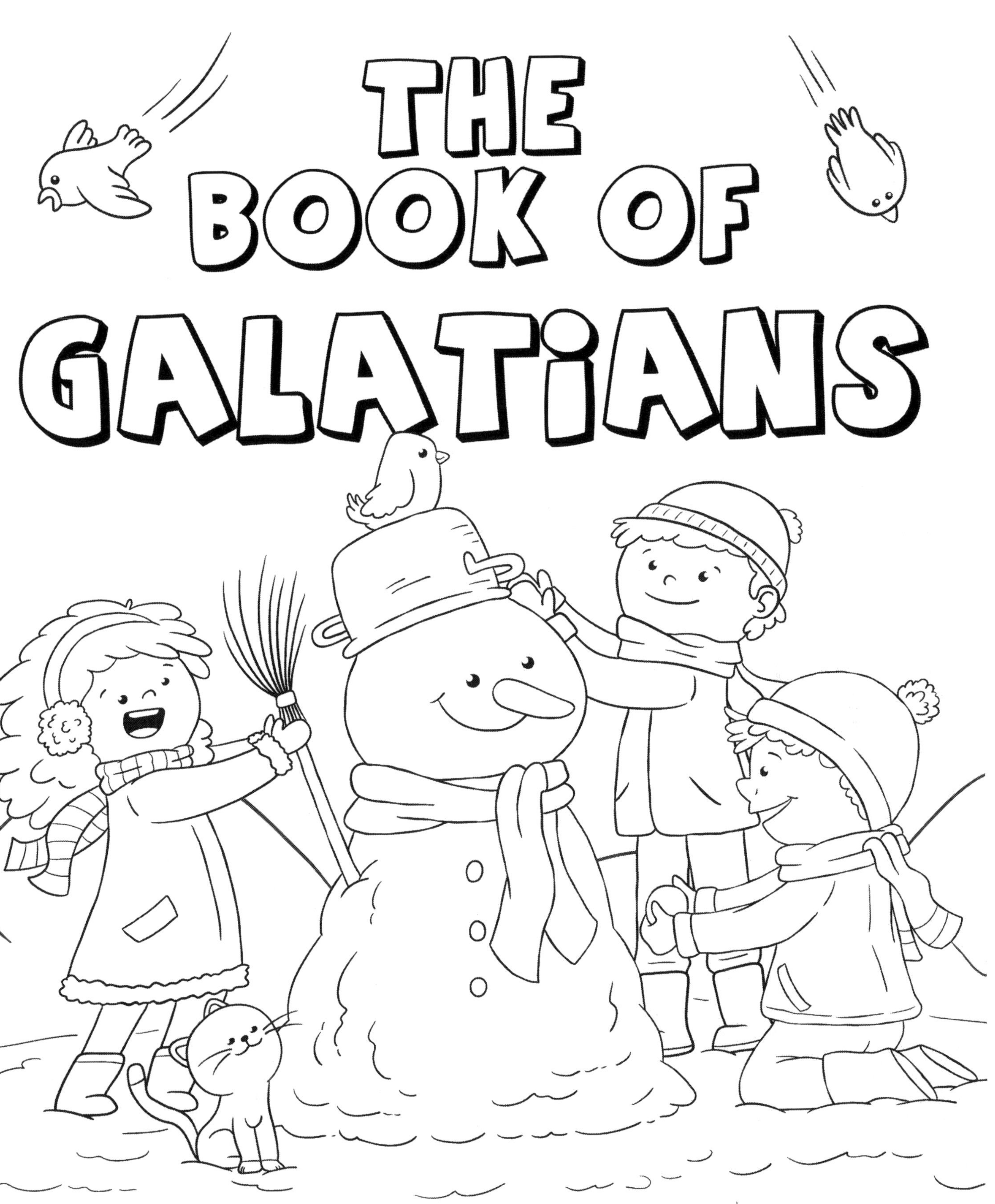
THE
BOOK OF
GALATiANS

This week we are learning about...

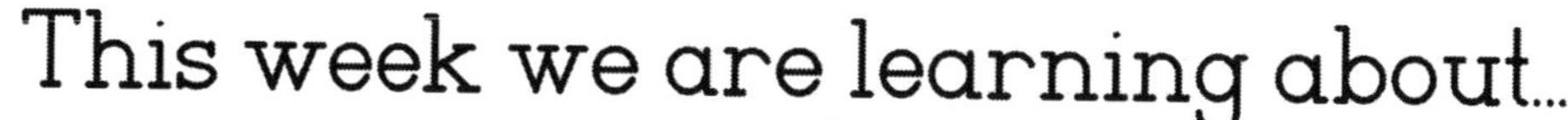

The Fruit of the Spirit

Have you ever heard about The Fruit of the Spirit? Maybe you've learned the song in Sunday School, but what is The Fruit of the Spirit and what does it mean?

In Galatians, Paul lists the nine specific behaviors that we as Christians should follow in our daily lives. It is also where the phrase "Fruit of the Spirit" comes from.

"But the fruit of the Spirit is love, joy, peace, forbearance, kindness, goodness, faithfulness, gentleness and self-control. Against such things there is no law."

- Galatians 5:22-23, NIV -

We use the word "fruit" as a metaphor for God's work in His people. In other words, Paul used the word to help us understand the work of The Holy Spirit in Christians.

A little bit confusing? Let's take a look at how fruit grows. It takes time after you plant the seed for it to mature. It doesn't just grow overnight. Just like The Fruit of the Spirit in our lives, it needs constant care from weeds and needs to be watered. As Christians, need to watch over ourselves, weeding out the sin in our lives that wants to take over. By following The Fruit of the Spirit, Christians are able to grow closer with God and stronger in our faith.

DAY ONE

Today's Date: ______________

In Galatians 5:22-23, love is translated from the Greek word γάπη, (agape). There are multiple words that the Greeks used to categorize love. Each has it's own individual meaning. Here are a few examples:

Storge - Although never used in the Bible, this love is used to describe the connection between family.

Philia - Love between friends.

Agape - The strongest and most cherished love, the love between God and His people.

Today we are going to be talking about the meaning of **Love**

Whoever does not love does not know God, because God **is love**

- 1 John 4:8, NIV -

The love of God is the strongest type of love you can feel. Do you remember when you accepted God into your heart?

If you've never asked God into your heart, you can find out how near the ending of this book.

____

____

What are some ways God has shown His love to you?

____

____

____

____

My prayer of the day...

Need ideas? Try, thank you, Lord for the love you give me everyday...

____

____

____

____

____

____

____

____

QUESTIONS I HAVE

Just a reminder that you can always ask a parent, friend or somone at church if you have any questions!

____

____

____

____

____

____

____

DAY TWO

Today's Date: ______________

Yesterday we talked about different types of love and we discused "agape," the everlasting love that God has with you.

Today we will be learning about joy. We often see joy in the Bible alongside happiness and gladness. Joy, in the sense that Paul is talking about, is the realization of God in your life. His grace and love brings joy to our lives. God fills us with joy.

Today we are going to be talking about the meaning of

Joy

Consider it pure joy, my brothers and sisters, whenever you face trials of many kinds, because you know that the testing of your faith produces perseverance.

- **James 1:2-3, NIV** -

Questions?

____

____

____

____

____

____

____

____

Fill in the blank scripture...

Look through your Bible and fill in the blanks for the scriptures talking about joy and peace. These are NIV.

John 16:33, NIV

"I have told you these things, so that in me you may have _ _ _ _ _ . In this world you will have _ _ _ _ _ _ _ . But take heart! I have overcome the _ _ _ _ _ ."

Romans 15:13, NIV

"May the _ _ _ of hope fill you with all joy and peace as you trust in him, so that you may _ _ _ _ _ _ _ _ with hope by the _ _ _ _ _ of the Holy Spirit."

Proverbs 12:20, NIV

"_ _ _ _ _ _ is in the hearts of those who plot evil, but those who _ _ _ _ _ _ _ peace have joy."

Today we are also talking about the meaning of

Peace

What exactly is peace? Peace is when you feel calm, stress-free, and secure. When we have God in our hearts we are filled with peace.

The mind governed by the flesh is death, but the mind governed by the Spirit is life and peace.

- Romans 8:6, NIV -

Activity of the day

LOVE JOY
PEACE GOD
FRUIT SPIRIT
FORBEARANCE
KINDNESS
GOODNESS
FAITHFULNESS
GENTLENESS
SELFCONTROL

N H Y S P I R P G D V I U S X
A O G S S E N D N I K I N F S
L M I U E P G O O D F G E A P
Y N A L H W I R S H I E O I R
L G O O D N E S S A C I R T A
O A K V G E L A T N D A F H L
V J O E D S E L A D I G U F O
F D I O L U A R R G E I Z U R
R V G Z P E A C E N I B C L T
U J O G U E C O T E P N R N N
I A Y P B E R L I U S H I E O
T R O R T W E G R L P Y A S C
B G O R T N O O I B A B O S F
R F S S E J D U P I A P A J L
V A F S A L O R S T N O C P E
A B S F R U E Q A N A F L E S

What I'm praying about today...

Need ideas? Try, "thank you Lord for..."
Maybe you can pray for someone in your life
who could use God's joy and peace in their lives?

DAY THREE Today's Date: ____________

Do you know what forbearance means? It's not commonly used but can be defined as patience. With God in our lives we are able to strengthen our fruit. Let's take a look at 1 Timothy 1:16 where Paul talks about Jesus' patience.

Today we are going to be talking about the meaning of

Forbearance

But for that very reason I was shown mercy so that in me, the worst of sinners, Christ Jesus might display his immense patience as an example for those who would believe in him and receive eternal life.

- 1 Timothy 1:16, NIV -

You can read through 1 Timothy 1:12-17 to learn more about the verse.

What are some ways you can be patient toward other people in your day-to-day life?

____

____

____

I am showing

Kindness by...

1. ______________________________
2. ______________________________
3. ______________________________
4. ______________________________

You probably know the meaning of kindness. It's being selfless and compassionate. It's a trait that we as Christians need to follow even though it can be hard. Ephesians 4:32 is a reminder for us to be kind.

"Be kind and compassionate to one another, forgiving each other, just as in Christ God forgave you."

- Ephesians 4:32, NIV -

Today we are also talking about the meaning of

Kindness

Activity of the day

Note: You can read through the last few pages for some of the answers

Down

1. Calm, stress-free and secure.

3. Chapter where Paul lists The Fruit of the Spirit.

4. You may know this verse, "Because of the Lord's great love we are not consumed, for his compassions never fail. They are new every morning; great is your _______." (Lamentations 3:22-23, NIV)

7. The realization of God in your life. God fills us with ___.

9. Known as "Agape." The first "fruit" Paul lists.

Across

2. "Surely your ________ and love will follow me all the days of my life, and I will dwell in the house of the Lord forever." (Psalm 23:6, NIV)

5. Can be defined as patience. It is what Jesus has in 1 Timothy 1:16, NIV.

6. Being selfless and compassionate.

8. The last "fruit" that Paul talks about in Galatians 5:22-23, NIV.

10. "Let your ________ be evident to all. The Lord is near." (Philippians 4:5, NIV)

What I'm praying about

Need ideas? Try praying for your church, those in need or your family and friends.

DAY FOUR

Today's Date: ____________

Today we are going to be talking about the meaning of

Goodness

Goodness is described as the quality of being good or virtuous. It is kindness of the heart. People are able to see goodness in us through our actions. But, what is the difference between goodness and kindness?

Kindness, like we discussed before, is being selfless and compassionate. Goodness, on the other hand is righteousness in action or doing what is right. They are two very important virtues to strengthen in your life.

They tell of the power of your awesome works – and I will proclaim your great deeds. They celebrate your abundant goodness and joyfully sing of your righteousness. The Lord is gracious and compassionate, slow to anger and rich in love.

- Psalm 145:6-8, NIV -

Today we are also talking about the meaning of

Faithfulness

Showing our faithfulness to God is important. It is one thing to believe in Him but another to be faithful to Him. But, what is being faithful?

It is a promise we give to God to always follow Him, to stay by His side and trust in Him through every step. To know and believe with your whole heart that He is the Lord, and to only follow Him.

The Lord rewards everyone for their righteousness and faithfulness. The Lord delivered you into my hands today, but I would not lay a hand on the Lord's anointed. 1 - Samuel 26:23, NIV.

My Prayer of the Day

Need ideas? "Lord, Help me to strengthen certain "fruit" such as…" "I thank you for…"

____

____

____

____

What are some good deeds I can do for people around me?

1. ______

2. ______

3. ______

What does being faithful mean to you?
How do you show your faithfulness to God?

______

Questions

______

DAY FIVE

Today's Date: ___________

Today we are going to be talking about the meaning of

Gentleness

Humble, calm, considerate, and kind. These are all words that can be used to describe gentleness. But why is gentleness so important to strength? We often see people who lack gentleness to be prideful, easily angered or revengeful. To be gentle is to be like Christ. Jesus talks about himself as being gentle in Matthew.

Take my yoke upon you and learn from me, for I am gentle and humble in heart, and you will find rest for your souls. - Matthew 11:29, NIV -

How can you show gentleness to others around you?

____

____

____

____

What are some ways that you can practice self-control?

____

____

____

____

Questions I have...

____

____

____

My Prayer

____

____

____

____

____

____

____

____

____

____

____

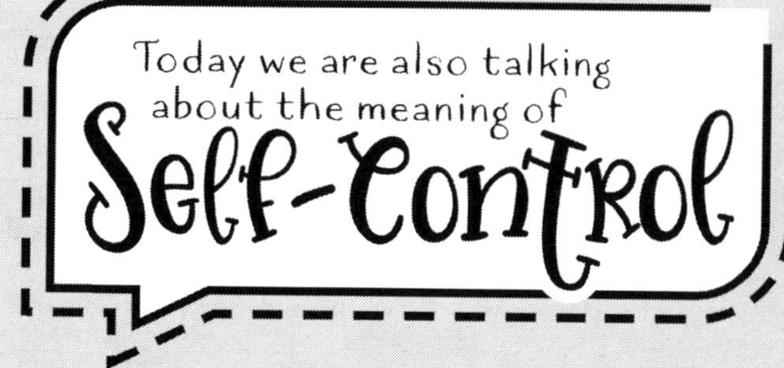

We all know about self-control, but why is it such an important "fruit?" Self-control is the ability to control one's self. By letting our desires take over we would quickly spiral out of control. With God we are able to strengthen ourselves. We are able to live a life with God and shut the door so sin can't creep through.

WHY ARE THE FRUIT OF THE SPIRIT IMPORTANT?

We've talked about the different fruit that Paul listed, but why are they so important? What is the true meaning and what is the purpose of the fruit?

"But the fruit of the Spirit is love, joy, peace, forbearance, kindness, goodness, faithfulness, gentleness and self-control. Against such things there is no law."

- Galatians 5:22-23, NIV -

In Galatians 5:22, when Paul talks about The Fruit of the Spirit, he is specifically referring to the Holy Spirit. The Holy Spirit leads and empowers Christians. With it we are able to grow into stronger, better people. Just like fruit that needs water to grow, the Holy spirit works to strengthen us. **"But you will receive power when the Holy Spirit comes on you"** - Acts 1:8, NIV. Not only do we use these to grow, we also use them to strengthen our relationship with Christ. As followers of Christ, it is important that we work to strengthen our relationship with God. It is the most important relationship that you will ever have.

"Submit yourselves, then, to God. Resist the devil, and he will flee from you. Come near to God and he will come near to you. Wash your hands, you sinners, and purify your hearts, you double-minded."

- James 4:7-8, NIV -

FILL IN THE BLANKS SCRIPTURE

Pick one of the "fruits" to fill in the blank.

Rejoice in the Lord always. I will say it again: Rejoice! Let your _____ be evident to all. The Lord is near. (Philippians 4:4-5, NIV)

May the Lord now show you _____ and faithfulness, and I too will show you the same favor because you have done this. (2 Samuel 2:6, NIV)

And the disciples were filled with _____ and with the Holy Spirit. (Acts 13:52, NIV)

Like a city whose walls are broken through is a person who lacks _____. (Proverbs 25:28, NIV)

"I have told you these things, so that in me you may have _____. In this world you will have trouble. But take heart! I have overcome the world." (John 16:33, NIV)

And the Lord said, "I will cause all my _____ to pass in front of you, and I will proclaim my name, the Lord, in your presence. I will have mercy on whom I will have mercy, and I will have compassion on whom I will have compassion. (Exodus 33:19, NIV)

Whoever does not love does not know God, because God is _____. (1 John 4:8, NIV)

They are new every morning; great is your _____. (Lamentations 3:23, NIV)

But the fruit of the Spirit is love, joy, peace, _____, kindness, goodness, faithfulness, gentleness and self-control. Against such things there is no law. (Galatians 5:22-23, NIV)

Love Joy Peace Forbearance Kindness
Goodness Faithfulness Gentleness Self-control

Be kind and compassionate
to one another, forgiving
each other just as in Christ God
forgave you
Ephesians 4:32, NIV

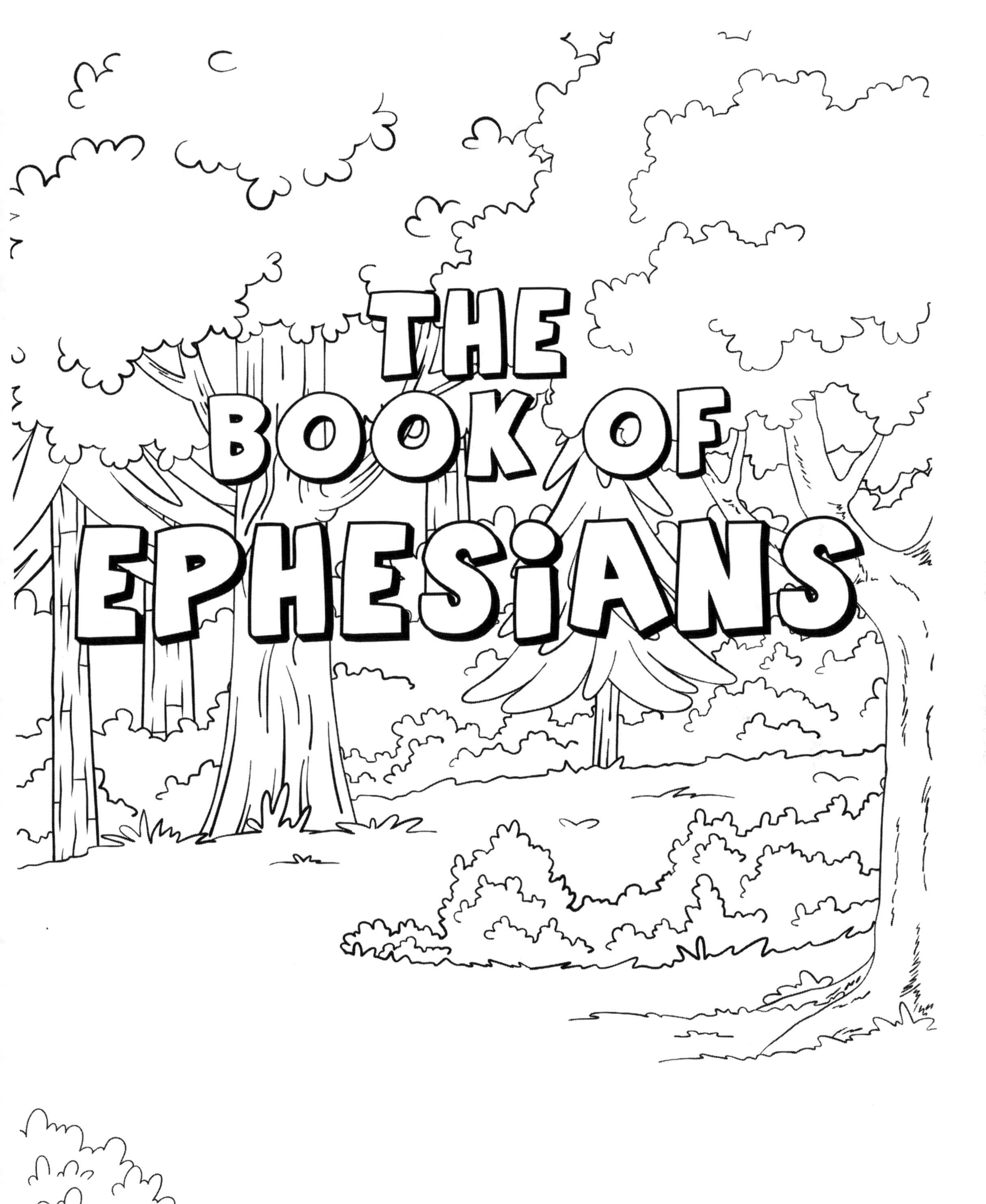
THE
BOOK OF
EPHESiANS

This week we are learning about...

The Armor of God

Have you ever heard about The Armor of God?
Soldiers in biblical days often wore heavy thick armor to battle.
In Ephesians, Paul talks about The Armor of God. It is the spiritual armor we wear as Christians in battle against the devil and his schemes.
So, how does it work, and how do you wear the armor?

It's very similar to The Fruit of the Spirit. By accepting God into your life you are able to strengthen yourself. When you imagine putting on the armor you are able to strengthen your relationship with God Who helps you to fight against the devil when he tries to tempt you and bring you down.

In the Bible, Paul tells us to put on The Full Armor of God, so that when the day of evil comes we are able so stand our guard and be ready. To wear The Full Armor we must wear: the belt of truth, the breastplate of righteousness, the shoes of peace, the shield of faith, the helmet of salvation, the sword of the spirit, and prayer. Let's take a look at what they mean in further detail...

SWORD OF THE SPIRIT

HELMET OF SALVATION

BREASTPLATE OF RIGHTEOUSNESS

SHIELD OF FAITH

THE BELT OF TRUTH

SHOES OF PEACE

PRAYER

DAY ONE

Today's Date: ____________

THE BELT OF TRUTH

The belt of truth is the first set of armor that Paul writes about, but what exactly does the belt of truth stand for, and why does he list it first, before the shield of faith or the sword of the spirit?

The belt was used for more than we think, it was one of the first pieces of armor that a soldier would put on. Used to protect the lower body, it also had a place to strap the breastplate on and held the scabbard (sword holder).

Just like the belt, truth is one of the first things we use to gear up. Without truth, we wouldn't be able to hold The Sword of the Spirit and The Breastplate of Righteousness would be loose. So, what is the meaning of truth?

As Christians, we need to make sure that we are always wearing truth. We need to be truthful and obey the truth of God's Word. **"The Lord detests lying lips, but he delights in people who are trustworthy."** (Proverbs 12:22, NIV)

Is obeying God's Word always easy? Why/Why not?

____

____

____

Is telling the truth always the right thing to do?

____

____

Have you ever told a lie? How did you feel afterwards?

____

____

Questions I have about The Belt of Truth: ______________________________

____

DAY TWO

Today's Date: ____________

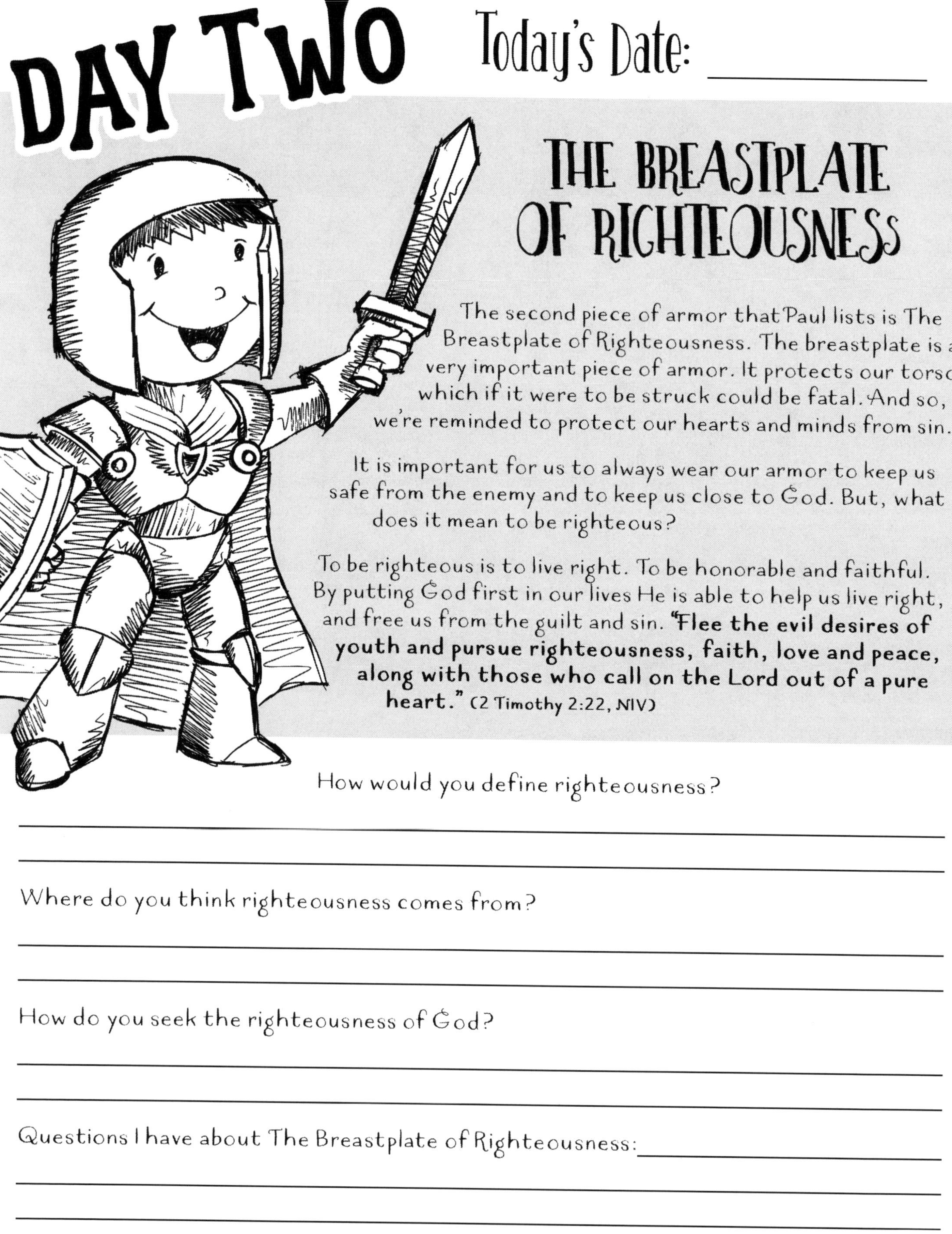

THE BREASTPLATE OF RIGHTEOUSNESS

The second piece of armor that Paul lists is The Breastplate of Righteousness. The breastplate is a very important piece of armor. It protects our torso, which if it were to be struck could be fatal. And so, we're reminded to protect our hearts and minds from sin.

It is important for us to always wear our armor to keep us safe from the enemy and to keep us close to God. But, what does it mean to be righteous?

To be righteous is to live right. To be honorable and faithful. By putting God first in our lives He is able to help us live right, and free us from the guilt and sin. **"Flee the evil desires of youth and pursue righteousness, faith, love and peace, along with those who call on the Lord out of a pure heart."** (2 Timothy 2:22, NIV)

How would you define righteousness?

____

____

Where do you think righteousness comes from?

____

____

How do you seek the righteousness of God?

____

____

Questions I have about The Breastplate of Righteousness: ____________

____

____

Feeding on the Word of God

DAY THREE Today's Date: ____________

SHOES OF PEACE

Have you ever walked outside without shoes? Maybe you don't think shoes are very important but they do indeed serve a very powerful purpose. The shoes of peace are the third piece of armor that we are going to talk about, but what do the shoes of peace mean?

Imagine being a soldier running through a battlefield over twigs and rocks, you would definitely need some shoes to protect yourself. Shoes allow us to step freely as we keep our minds focused on the battle. The Bible tells us to stand firm with our gospel shoes on. What this is saying is that we need to stand firm in our faith. Stand firm when you're happy, stand firm when you're sad. Don't give up on God when you have a tough day. Don't follow others who don't believe the same way as you. Hold on to what you believe and don't let anyone tell you you're wrong.

In the same way that soldiers wear combat boots, soldiers of faith must be ready to fight with the right pair of shoes. The right pair of shoes in this case is The Gospel of Peace. What better shoes could we ever hope to receive than shoes made by God? And what are those shoes? They're called gospel shoes because the words in the Bible are what help us stand strong. When we read the Bible we have the strength that we need to be good soldiers of faith.

He said to them, "Go into all the world and preach the **gospel** to all creation.
Mark 16:15, NIV

My Prayer of The Day

____

____

____

____

What should you do if someone tells you not to believe in God?

Do you think it's important to read the Bible everyday? Why or why not?

What are Gospel Shoes?

Can you think of anyone in the Bible that stood strong in tough times?
(Hint: He fed 5,000 people with a loaf of bread and 5 fish in Matthew 14:13-21)

Questions I have about The Shoes of Peace:

Can you find your way through the maze

Note: Start from the top of the shoe and end here at the bottom

DAY FOUR

Today's Date: ______________

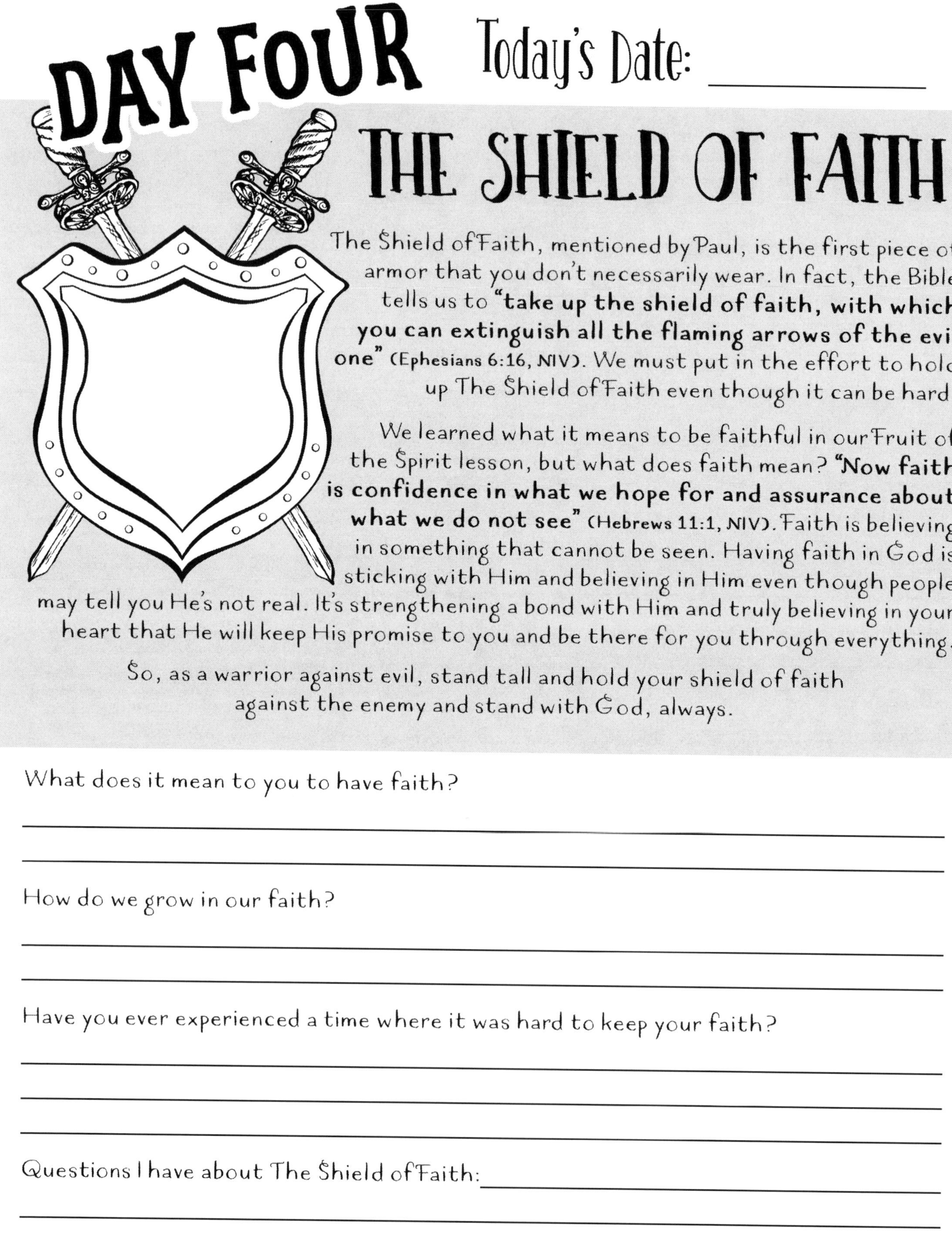

THE SHIELD OF FAITH

The Shield of Faith, mentioned by Paul, is the first piece of armor that you don't necessarily wear. In fact, the Bible tells us to **"take up the shield of faith, with which you can extinguish all the flaming arrows of the evil one"** (Ephesians 6:16, NIV). We must put in the effort to hold up The Shield of Faith even though it can be hard.

We learned what it means to be faithful in our Fruit of the Spirit lesson, but what does faith mean? **"Now faith is confidence in what we hope for and assurance about what we do not see"** (Hebrews 11:1, NIV). Faith is believing in something that cannot be seen. Having faith in God is sticking with Him and believing in Him even though people may tell you He's not real. It's strengthening a bond with Him and truly believing in your heart that He will keep His promise to you and be there for you through everything.

So, as a warrior against evil, stand tall and hold your shield of faith against the enemy and stand with God, always.

What does it mean to you to have faith?

____

____

How do we grow in our faith?

____

____

Have you ever experienced a time where it was hard to keep your faith?

____

____

____

Questions I have about The Shield of Faith: ______________________________

____

____

Activity of the day

ARMOR
SHOES
SOLDIER
SPIRIT
BELT
TRUTH
SWORD
PRAYER
PEACE
SHIELD
FAITH
HELMET
BREASTPLATE
RIGHTEOUSNESS
SALVATION

E	B	R	E	A	S	T	P	L	A	T	E	U	S	X
H	S	G	S	B	E	N	D	L	O	S	I	A	H	S
P	M	S	T	E	P	G	O	O	D	F	L	S	O	A
T	N	A	E	R	W	I	R	S	H	I	E	O	I	L
R	S	T	O	N	U	E	T	S	H	I	E	L	D	V
U	P	K	R	G	S	T	A	T	E	N	A	D	H	A
P	I	O	S	U	S	U	H	A	L	W	O	I	F	T
E	R	I	O	W	U	A	O	U	M	S	H	E	U	I
A	I	A	R	M	O	R	O	E	E	I	W	R	L	O
C	T	B	E	L	E	E	O	F	T	P	N	R	H	N
E	A	R	P	Y	W	S	L	A	U	H	E	I	E	O
T	R	E	A	S	E	E	T	I	L	P	G	R	S	C
F	G	R	H	O	N	M	O	T	B	A	G	I	B	F
A	P	P	H	E	R	D	U	H	E	A	I	A	R	L
I	R	S	P	A	S	W	O	R	D	N	A	S	P	E
A	B	S	F	R	U	T	L	E	B	A	F	L	E	S

What I'm praying for today...

Need ideas? Try praying for those who are sick, or ask for guidance and wisdom for yourself or someone you know.

Who is it that overcomes the world? Only the one who believes that Jesus is the Son of God

- 1 John 5:5, NIV -

DAY FIVE

Today's Date: ____________

THE HELMET OF SALVATION

The Helmet of Salvation mentioned in Ephesians (New Testament) was also mentioned in the Old Testament in The Book of Isaiah. It talks about how God wore The Breastplate and The Helmet of Salvation. **"He put on righteousness as his breastplate, and the helmet of salvation on his head; he put on the garments of vengeance and wrapped himself in zeal as in a cloak"** (Isaiah 59:17, NIV).

We need to wear the armor just as God has and does. But, what does it mean to wear The Helmet of Salvation?

A life with salvation is to be saved from a life of sin and death. So, how do we receive salvation? The Bible says **"For it is by grace you have been saved, through faith—and this is not from yourselves, it is the gift of God"** (Ephesians 2:8, NIV). By faith we are able to receive salvation, but salvation cannot be earned. It is a gift that God gives to his people who repent from their sin and believe in Him. It is the most important gift that God can give you. As you wear your helmet you need to keep your mind clear from sin and focus on only God's Word and what His plans are for your life. Follow Him, and stay faithful through everything.

Can anyone have salvation? What does God ask of you?

____

____

____

What are some things you are doing to grow closer with God?

____

____

Questions I have about the Helmet of Salvation: ____________________

____

Salvation
has come for all.

DAY SIX

Today's Date: ____________

THE SWORD OF THE SPIRIT

Can you name a single knight that didn't use a sword? Without our sword we are pretty much defenseless. Armor may have pieces that seem more important than others but that's not true, as we learned about in shoes of peace. All the armor is vital for fighting, and not a single piece can be left out.

While all the armor is valuable, the sword is the one piece that allows us to attack. It is the only weapon that Paul mentions. With God's Word as our sword we are able to conquer any sin that stands in our way. Ephesians tells us that The Sword of the Spirit is The Word of God. **"Take the helmet of salvation and the sword of the Spirit, which is the word of God."**

(Ephesians 6:17, NIV)

What Bible story do you know where the main character used the Word of God to defeat evil? (See Matthew 4:1-11)

____

____

____

____

Is there any temptation we can't defeat when we use The Sword of the Spirit?

____

____

As soldiers, in order to practice using the sword we must study the Word of God. We must study the Word in order to strengthen it in our hearts. Studying and reading are two different things, to study is to understand it's true meaning.
What are some ways you are studying God's Word?

____

____

____

Questions I have about The Sword of the Spirit: ____________________

____

____

Activity of the day

Armor of God crossword

(All answers are in the book unless you need to look up a verse.)

Down

2. The last "armor" Paul mentions.

3. To stay far away from lies.

5. The ____ of truth.

7. The _____ of the spirit.

8. ______ of faith.

9. ______ of salvation.

11. _____ of peace.

12. Believing in something that cannot be seen.

Across

1. The Sword of the ______.

4. ___________ of righteousness.

6. To be saved from a life of sin and death.

10. To live right, honorable and faithful.

13. "Make every effort to live in _____ with everyone and to be holy; without holiness no one will see the Lord." **(Hebrews 12:14, NIV)**

DAY SEVEN Today's Date: ____________

AND FINALLY, PRAYER

This past week we've talked about the different armor of God. Today we will be talking about prayer, something Paul adds in his description of the armor. Paul also goes on to say in Ephesians, **"And pray in the Spirit on all occasions with all kinds of prayers and requests. With this in mind, be alert and always keep on praying for all the Lord's people."** (Ephesians 6:18, NIV)

As we've been reading, we cannot use the armor without every piece working together. Prayer is not a piece of armor, but still very important. As Christians wearing the armor we are not able to use it if God is not present in it.

Prayer is our way of communicating with God. It's our way of connecting with Him and it is a very special thing. Without prayer (talking with God) it would be impossible to use your armor well to defeat Satan.

When we pray to God we can talk about anything!
What are some things you usually talk to God about?

____

____

____

Now that we've gone over The Armor of God, what was your favorite part and why?

____

____

____

What have you learned about The Armor of God?

____

____

____

Questions I have about prayer: ____________________

____

____

My Prayer of The Day

Need ideas? Try praying for someone you know, or thank God for something He's done.

___

___

___

___

___

SINNERS PRAYER

Would you like to be a Christian?
Would you like to invite Jesus into your heart?

The Bible tells us that Salvation is a free gift from God. He invites everyone who believes in Jesus into the family of God, but He also asks us to turn away from a life of sin. And so, this prayer is a starting point of a new life with Jesus. Let's ask Him to forgive our sins, as we invite Jesus into our lives.

DEAR HEAVENLY FATHER,

THANK YOU FOR YOUR FREE GIFT OF SALVATION.
I'M SORRY FOR ALL OF THE BAD THINGS I HAVE DONE.
PLEASE FORGIVE ME FOR ALL OF MY SINS,
AND HELP ME TO LIVE A NEW LIFE THAT SERVES YOU.

I BELIEVE THAT JESUS IS LORD AND THAT HE DIED
ON THE CROSS TO PAY FOR MY SINS.

I ASK THAT JESUS WILL COME INTO MY HEART.
I'M ASKING HIM TO BE IN CHARGE OF MY LIFE.
TO BE WITH ME ALWAYS AND TO HELP ME MAKE GOOD CHOICES.

IN THE NAME OF JESUS, I PRAY, AMEN.

Congratulations, you have just accepted God's free gift of Salvation.
Make sure that you take this prayer seriously by living a life that is pleasing to God.

The Bible also tells us that we should be baptized. Baptism is our way of showing the world that we belong to Jesus. If you haven't been baptized yet, maybe you can talk to your parents so that together you can choose a good time to do that.

GLOSSARY

A

Altar
An altar is a raised structure where people are able to offer gifts and offerings to God.

Amalekite
A member of the tribe of Amalek. *"Esau's son Eliphaz also had a concubine named Timna, who bore him Amalek. These were grandsons of Esau's wife Adah."* (Genesis 36:12, NIV)

Ark
The type of boat that Noah built during for the flood.

Armor of God
The spiritual armor we wear as Christians in battle against the devil and his schemes.

B

Babel "Tower of Babel"
Named Babel after God gave everyone a new language and confused them so they could no longer understand each other and continue making their tower.

Banquet
A get together, usually a meal, in honor or recognition of a particular person. Banquets can be large and extravagant.

Book of the Chronicles of the Kings
A book with records detailing the kings and special events that took place during their reigns.

Burnt offerings
An offering to God that is burned on an altar.

C

Clean / Unclean Animals
Clean Animals - These were animals like sheep and cows that Jewish people could eat. This diet set the Jews apart from other people.

Unclean Animals - These were animals that Jewish people wouldn't eat, like pigs or owls.

Commandments "Ten Commandments"
Set of principles and rules that God has given to Christians to follow. Ways we can grow closer with God.

Covenant
Another word for agreement.

Cubits
A cubit was a common measurement used in the Bible. It was roughly the distance from your fingertip down to your elbow. A cubit was estimated to be around 18 inches.

D

Decree
Another way to describe a legal order.

Disciple
A follower of Jesus.

E

Elders
An elder is a person who is older than you. This person is usually valued for their wisdom and is known to be responsible and hold authority.

Eunuch
A special guard trained to protect the women's living areas. A man who is fully trusted to focus on his job without being distracted by the beautiful women. King's would be able to trust these men with their queens, princesses and their attendants.

F

Fasting
Fasting is when a person gives up something they commonly use to show God that all we need is Him. Most commonly people fast by not eating or drinking. It is a symbol that we are putting God first.

Fruit of the Spirit
In Galatians, Paul lists the nine specific behaviors that we as Christians should follow so that we are able to grow closer with God and stronger in our Christianity.

H

Harem
It was the private space for the women to stay, or the group of women who stayed there.

Hebrew
A Hebrew was typically referred to as a descendant of Abraham, Issac, and Jacob who were introduced to us in Genesis.

I

Idols
An Idol is either an image or object that people use to worship as a god. In Exodus, Aaron built a gold statue of a calf to worship, this would considered an idol.

Israelites
Descendants of Jacob are referred to as Israelites because in Genesis 32:27-28, Jacob's name was changed to "Israel."

J

Jew
Descendants of Israel (also called Jacob)

L

Leprous "Leprosy"
Leprous is a way of saying someone has leprosy. It is an infection caused by bacteria that affects the skin.

Lots (Casting Lots)
Casting lots was a method people used to determine the "will of God". They used either sticks or stones with markings and threw them into a small area where the results were interpreted.

M

Midwives
A midwife is a professional that is trained to help pregnant women through their pregnancy and may also help deliver babies.

N

Nobles
Someone who has noble ranking from birth. Known to be wealthy and powerful.

O

Offerings
Special gifts of personal value that people offer to God. Cain and Abel for example offered livestock and grains.

P

Parable
A story that is used to teach a lesson. Jesus often used parables when talking with others.

Pharaoh
Pharaoh is the common title used for the monarchs of ancient Egypt.

Plagues
Destructive and widespread, a plague can come in many forms. Sickness, death, or anything that causes extreme annoyance such as bugs can all be part of a plague. In Exodus we see how God put plagues on Egypt to show his power to them.

Proclamation
An important official announcement.

Prophet
A person who delivers messages from God. A well known prophet we've talked about is Moses and another is Jonah.

R

Recede
For something to move back further from its previous position. God caused the waters to recede in Genesis during the flood.

S

Sabbath
A day of rest

Sackcloth
A coarsely woven fabric. It was symbolized as a sign of submission of humility before God.

Sacred
Something sharing a connection with God. In Moses and the burning bush God calls the ground that Moses is standing on sacred.

Satraps
The governor of a province during Biblical times.

Signet Ring
Traditionally worn on the pinkie finger, this ring was used to seal a document. Signet rings were usually used for royal documents and no document written in the king's name and sealed with his ring could be revoked.

Sorcerer
Men who practiced witchcraft.

T

Tax Collector
A person who gained personal wealth by collecting taxes. They were not very well liked during these times.

V

Vault
The open space in the sky.

W

Walked with God
To agree with God and live the way He wants you to.

Wise Men
A magician or person who claimed to have magic powers. They were also fortune tellers of a sort. These were different from the wise men who followed the star to see Jesus. Those men were likely kings.

ANSWER KEY ...... OLD TESTAMENT

The Book of Genesis

The Beginning - Day 1

Noah and the Ark - Day 2

Down	Across
1. Genesis	3. Noah
2. Japheth	5. Altar
4. Ham	7. Shem
6. Rainbow	8. Ark
9. Raven	10. Cubit
11. Flood	12. Dove
	13. Wind

The Book of Exodus

The Birth of Moses - Day 1

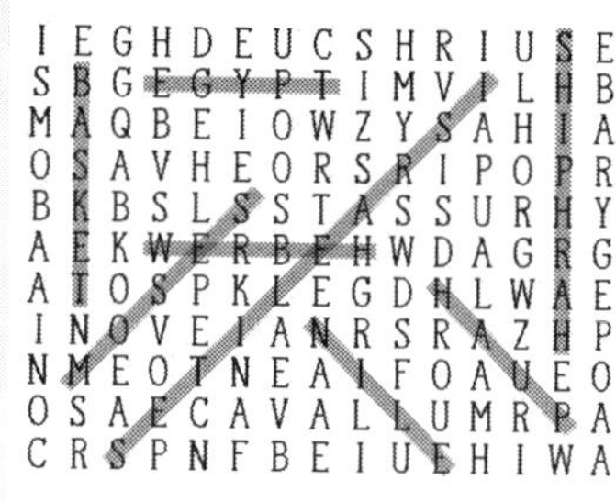

Moses and the Burning Bush - Day 1

Down	Across
1. Fire	2. Moses
3. Mountain	7. Pharaoh
4. Egypt	9. Elders
5. Bush	
6. Sandals	
8. Cry	

Ten Plagues of Egypt - Day 3

S B R E A S T P N A T E U S L
E S G S B E N D I O S I A I S
S M S T A F F O L D F L C O A
O N A E R W I R E H H E O I L
M S T O N U E T S H A E L D K
U P K R G S T A T E I A D H C
P H A R A O H H A L L O F F O
E R I O W L A N U M S H L U T
A I A R M O O O E E I W I L S
C T B E L R E C F T S N E H E
E F R P A W S L U N H E S E V
D R E A S E E T A S P G R S I
F O R H O N M K T B T G I B L
A G O H E R E U H E A S A R L
I S S L A S W O S L I O B P E
A B S F B U T L E B A F L E S

Ten Plagues of Egypt - Day 6

Down	Across
1. Donkey	2. Frogs
3. Blood	5. Flies
4. Plague	6. Aaron
7. Pray	10. Snake
8. Israelites	12. Egyptians
9. Livestock	14. Magicians
11. Staff	15. Moses
13. Pharaoh	17. Goshen
16. Seven	19. Gnats
18. Dust	

Ten Plagues of Egypt - Day 7

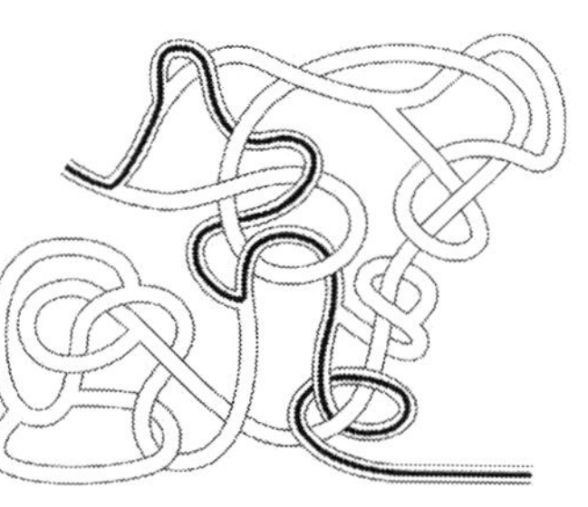

Ten Plagues of Egypt - Day 9

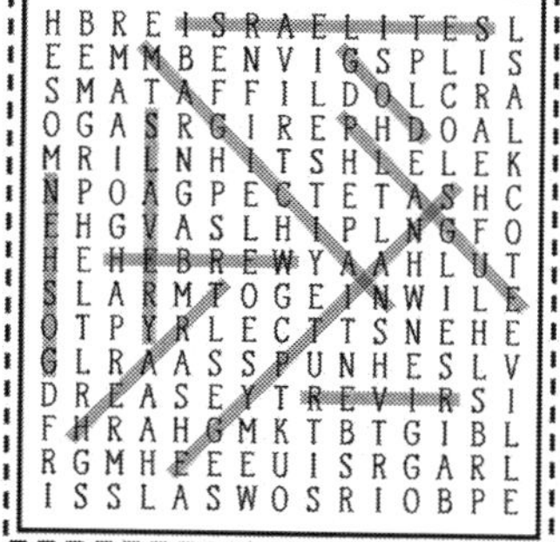

Ten Commandments - Day 2

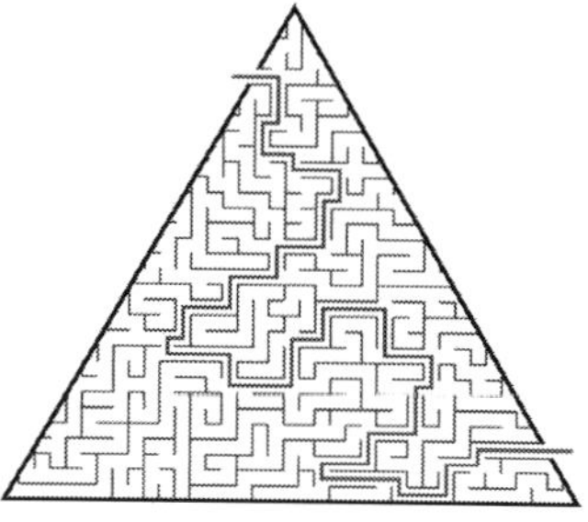

Ten Commandments - Day 3

Break The Code

In fact, this is love for God: to keep his commands. And his commands are not burdensome.

- 1 John 5:3 -

I will extol thee, my God, O king; and I will bless thy name for ever and ever.

- Psalm 145:1 -

Ten Commandments - Day 4

Down	Across
1. Respect	2. Parents
4. Steal	3. Lie
6. Sinai	5. Tablets
7. Jealous	8. Marriage
9. Moses	10. Kill
12. God	11. Rest
13. Fake	14. Commandments
15. Exodus	18. Trumpets
16. Fire	
17. Forty	

Ten Commandments - Day 6

Match the Commandment

1st - Third Commandment
2nd - Fifth Commandment
3rd - Seventh Commandment
4th - Second Commandment
5th - Sixth Commandment
6th - Tenth Commandment
7th - First Commandment
8th - Ninth Commandment
9th - Fourth Commandment
10th - Eight Commandment

Ten Commandments - Day 8

Ten Commandments - Day 9

Break The Code

No one who practices deceit will dwell in my house; no one who speaks falsely will stand in my presence.

- Psalm 101:7 -

Then you will know the truth, and the truth will set you free.

- John 8:32 -

The Book of Esther

Esther - Day 2

Esther - Day 3

Bible Trivia

1st - C	**8th** - A
2nd - B	**9th** - C
3rd - I	**10th** - D
4th - C	**11th** - A
5th - G	**12th** - I
6th - H & E	**13th** - F
7th - C	

OLD TESTAMENT PAGE 2

Esther - Day 5

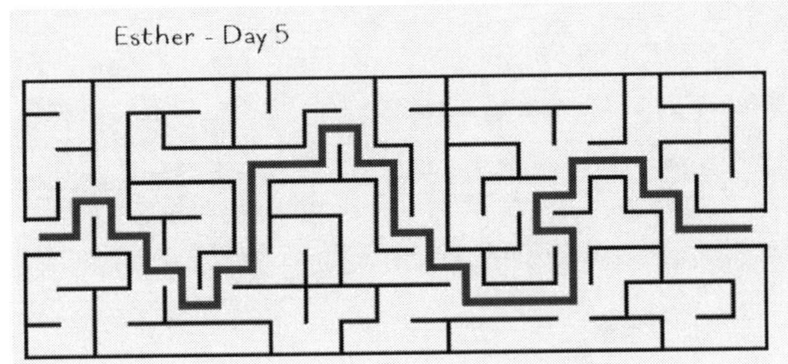

Esther - Day 5

Down

2. Crown
3. Twelve
4. Cousins
7. Bigthana
9. Harem
10. Mordecai
11. Hadassah
13. Vashti
14. Sackcloth
16. Eunuch
19. Haman
22. Death

Across

1. Scepter
5. Zeresh
6. Queen
8. Hegai
12. Gold
15. Teresh
17. Ahasuerus
18. Susa
20. Kill
21. Hathak
23. Fast
24. Amalekite
25. Banquet

Esther - Day 7

Bible Trivia

1st - G
2nd - F
3rd - B
4th - C
5th - F
6th - B
7th - D
8th - F
9th - E
10th - C
11th - A
12th - B

The Book of Daniel

Daniel - Day 1

A E O W D E U C S E R I U S X
N K G O D P O A I M V D L R B
J I Q U E C O W Z Y S A H O I
Y N A V H W O R S H I P O K R
F D B L L J S T D A R I R T A
Y A K I G F L A T W D A G U D
A W O R P K R E G D A L W S Q
R N Z V E I A L R N R P Z D P
P M E O C N E A T F I A C E O
O K A C C I V O L B U K R C A
C R M P N F R E I U S H I W A
P R A A Z E T G A L I O A A C
X E D R I N O L Y B A B I L U
R E S C U G D U A R P W B A A

Daniel - Day 2

Down

2. Daniel
3. Shut
4. Three
6. Babylon
8. Law
10. Joy

Across

1. Darius
5. Punished
7. Faithful
9. Angel
11. Lions

The Book of Jonah

Jonah - Day 3

Down

1. Praying
3. Tarshish
6. Swallowed
8. Sackcloth
9. Old-Testament
10. Proclamation
12. Joppa
14. Three

Across

2. Boat
4. Sleeping
5. Fish
7. Sea
11. Lots
13. Jonah
15. Gath-Hepher
16. Nineveh

NEW TESTAMENT

The Book of Luke

Birth of Jesus - Day 1

N A G A B R I E L I U S J
J M S E J D J R P J P E E
O E A O G O E D F E R N L
H R A R H R N N M S E G I
O P B N Y S A A J U G A Z
A L G J O B Z N E S N H A
N E D E N G A G E D A F B
S G L E A R R B E M N U E
A N G N A E E N Y B T L T
O A U E B R T E A N B N H
E J O S E P H B S O J A M
O R J A E R U O I V A S G

Birth of Jesus - Day 2

Down

1. Pregnant
3. Manger
4. Joseph
6. Angel

Across

2. Mary
5. Saviour
7. Jesus
8. Bethlehem
9. Shepherds

Birth of Jesus - Day 3

Bible Trivia

1st - C
2nd - E
3rd - H
4th - A
5th - J
6th - B
7th - F & G
8th - C
9th - I
10th - G
11th - D
12th - L
13th - D
14th - A
15th - H
16th - K

Zacchaeus - Day 1

Z J R E I S R A E S T G E S E
E A E S W E N N I U S R L J S
S M C R I E F I T S D L E R A
H J A C I N A R E E H I O E L
O E I L N C I L B J L E L N K
R R W E A E H M T C T A W N C
T T G V J S I O I H L N G I O
H C L E B L E R T A Y A O S T
S Z A C C H A E U S N H E L E
I E P T R L C C T I S N E W E

The Book of John

Water to Wine - Day 1

The Lost Sheep - Day 1

G U Y A O I A S G L U I I S
R J G H S E A P E E H S Z I
Q E M U N P C O W D F G B N
Y A P L U K E R E P E E J N
L J O E D N E S S E C I R E F
O E K V N E L A L N D A F R L
V S S T D T S B N D S G T S O
F U I O L U A R R O E T K U L
R S U Z P R A A P N S Y C L T
U J L G A E C U T E R S R R N
I E Y P B E R L I O S H E E O
T R O R T R E G T L P T A L C
B G S H E N O S I B A B H S F

The Lost Sheep - Day 2

Down

1. Astray
2. Voice
3. Sovereign
4. Justice
9. Lord

Across

5. Rejoicing
6. Sheep
7. Repent
8. Eternal
10. God

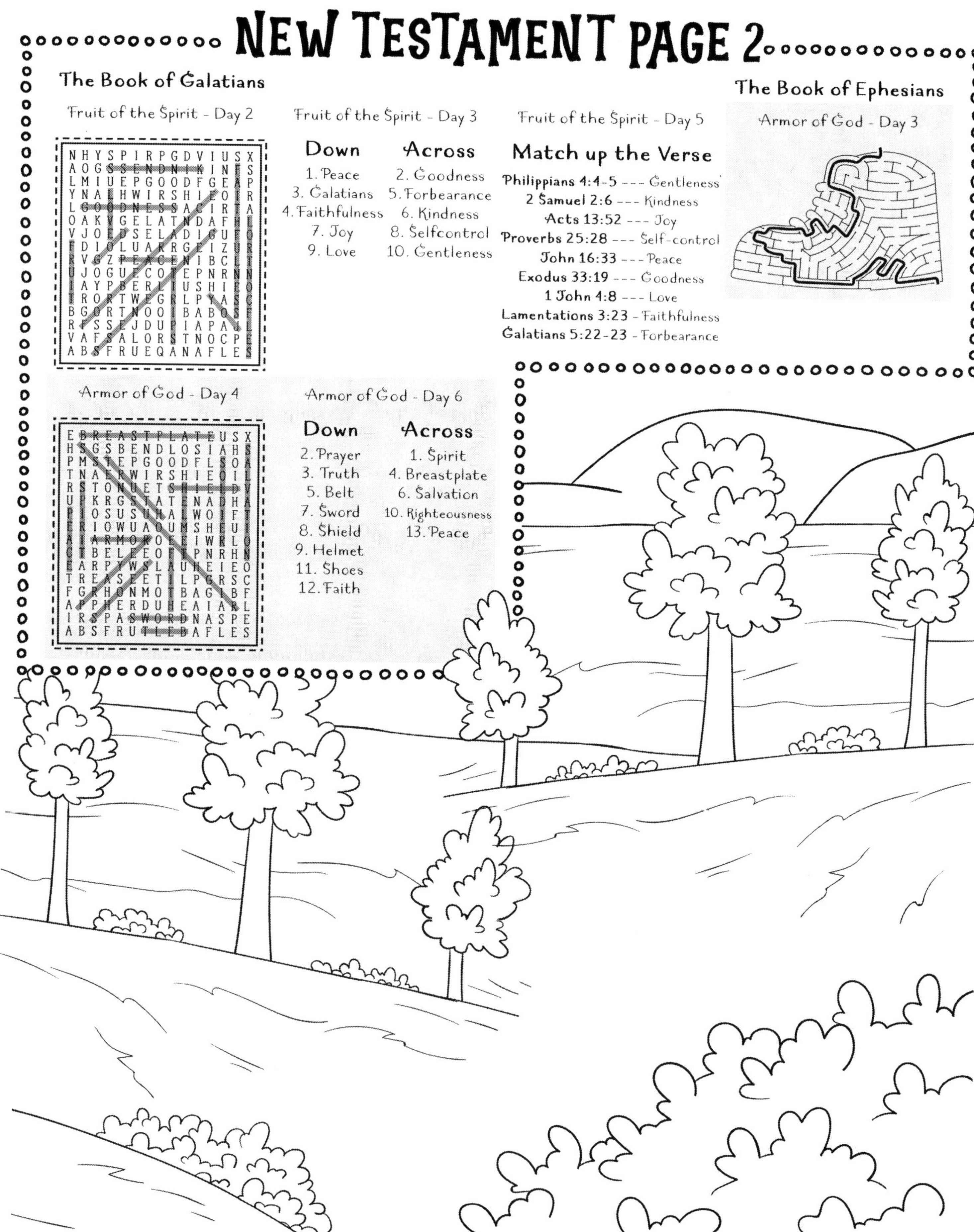
NEW TESTAMENT PAGE 2
The Book of Galatians
Fruit of the Spirit - Day 2
Fruit of the Spirit - Day 3
Down
1. Peace
3. Galatians
4. Faithfulness
7. Joy
9. Love
Across
2. Goodness
5. Forbearance
6. Kindness
8. Selfcontrol
10. Gentleness
Fruit of the Spirit - Day 5
Match up the Verse
Philippians 4:4-5 --- Gentleness
2 Samuel 2:6 --- Kindness
Acts 13:52 --- Joy
Proverbs 25:28 --- Self-control
John 16:33 --- Peace
Exodus 33:19 --- Goodness
1 John 4:8 --- Love
Lamentations 3:23 - Faithfulness
Galatians 5:22-23 - Forbearance
The Book of Ephesians
Armor of God - Day 3
Armor of God - Day 4
Armor of God - Day 6
Down
2. Prayer
3. Truth
5. Belt
7. Sword
8. Shield
9. Helmet
11. Shoes
12. Faith
Across
1. Spirit
4. Breastplate
6. Salvation
10. Righteousness
13. Peace

Made in the USA
Columbia, SC
16 March 2023